R U I N E D   B Y   R E A D I N G

RUINED BY

A LIFE IN BOOKS

READING

Lynne Sharon Schwartz

BEACON PRESS

BOSTON

Beacon Press
25 Beacon Street
Boston, Massachusetts 02108-2892

BEACON PRESS BOOKS
are published under the auspices of
the Unitarian Universalist Association of Congregations.

01 00 99 98 97 96   8 7 6 5 4

Library of Congress Cataloging-in-Publication Data

Schwartz, Lynne Sharon.
Ruined by reading : a life in books /
Lynne Sharon Schwartz.
p. cm.
ISBN 0-8070-7082-3
1. Schwartz, Lynne Sharon — Biography. I. Title.
PS3569.C567Z88   1996
813'.54 — dc20
[B]   95-43482

RUINED BY READING

⟨❦⟩ RARELY does the daily paper move me to re-examine my life. But a recent *New York Times* piece quoted a Chinese scholar whose "belief in Buddhism . . . has curbed his appetite for books." Mr. Cha says, "To read more is a handicap. It is better to keep your own mind free and to not let the thinking of others interfere with your own free thinking." I clipped his statement and placed it on the bedside table, next to a pile of books I was reading or planned to read or thought I ought to read. The clipping is about two square inches and almost weightless, the pile of books some nine inches high, weighing a few pounds. Yet they face each other in perfect balance. I am the scale on which they rest.

Lying in the shadow of the books, I brood on my reading habit. What is it all about? What am I doing it for? And the classic addict's question, What is it doing for me? Mr. Cha's serenity and independence of mind are enviable. I would like to be equally independent, but I'm not sure my mind could be free without reading, or that the action books have on it is properly termed "interference." I suspect the interaction of the mind and the book is something more complex. I can see it encompassing an intimate history and geography: the evolution of character, the shifting map of personal taste. And what about the uses of language itself, as well as the perennial lure of narrative? But perhaps casting the issue in such large terms only shows how enslaved I am. Buddhism aside, there is no Readers Anonymous, so far, to help curb this appetite.

Luckily I am not prey to every kind of reading, for there are many kinds, as there are many kinds of love, not all of them intoxicating. There is pure and specific curiosity: how would an Israeli Arab regard growing up in an inhospitable state, or who was Albertine, really, or what is it like to be brilliantly gifted and in love and desperately ill at twenty-three years old? Then we don't read directly for the "high," though we may find it, in Anton Shammas's *Arabesques* or Keats's letters, but to satisfy the mind. Or less specific curiosity: What is anthropology, I used to wonder — the enterprise itself, not the exotic data, since ordinary urban life provides enough exotic data. How do you approach the study of "man" or "culture"? How do you tilt your head, what angle of vision? I read enough to find out how the discipline works, which is by accumulation and accretion, making a mosaic. You gather and place enough pieces, then step back and look. I saw the pattern most luminously in Ruth Benedict's brilliant study, *Patterns of Culture*, which still sits stalwartly on my shelf in its thirty-five-cent Penguin paperback edition, the pages going brown but not yet flaking, still viable, still credible. Even from the old-fashioned précis under each chapter heading I sensed that here I would find what I wanted: "Man moulded by custom, not instinct"; "All standards of behavior relative"; "Peoples who never heard of war"; "Death, the paramount affront." Irresistible. I read, there and elsewhere, and when the design was clear to me, I stopped.

We may read for facts alone: the eye skims along, alert for key words, and when they appear, like red lights on a highway, it slides deftly to a halt. That kind of reading propelled me out of graduate school. However useful, it does not feel like true reading but more like shopping, riffling through racks for the precise shade of blue. I would have made a poor and ludicrous scholar, like a diva singing ditties in TV commercials, or a pastry chef condemned to macrobiotic menus.

My addiction is to works of the imagination, and even if I became a Buddhist, I think I couldn't renounce them cold turkey. Not after a lifetime, the better part of which was spent reading. Was it actually the better part, though? Did I choose or was I chosen, shepherded into it like those children caught out early on with a talent for the violin or ballet, baseball or gymnastics, and tethered forever to bows and barres, bats and mats? We didn't know any alternatives; there was no chance to find them out. Reading, of all these, does not win huge sums of money or applause, or give joy and solace to others. What it does offer is a delectable exercise for the mind, and Mr. Cha, the Buddhist scholar, might well find it an indulgence. Like the bodies of dancers or athletes, the minds of readers are genuinely happy and self-possessed only when cavorting around, doing their stretches and leaps and jumps to the tune of words.

Despite all this mental pirouetting, or maybe because of it, I don't remember much of what I've read. My lifelong capacity for forgetting distresses me. I glance at a book on the shelf that I once read with avid interest — Dorothy Gallagher's *All the Right Enemies*, about the 1943 murder of the Italian anarchist Carlo Tresca — and while I struggle for the details, all I recall is the excitement of the reading. I couldn't give a cogent account of its dense intrigue or social history, yet I have some inchoate sense of the texture and dynamics of the subject.

At least I remember there was a murder at stake, something I can't always claim. When my younger daughter made disparaging remarks about *Billy Budd* I rushed to Melville's defense with a speech on the conflict between the rule of law applied generically and the merits of individual cases. Billy Budd struck a superior officer, I reminded her; according to the letter of the law, he must hang. And yet, and yet, we cannot quite swallow it . . . I ended in a glow of ambivalence. "It wasn't that he struck him," she murmured. "He killed him." I had totally forgotten, which was appalling. And yet, I consoled myself, I had remembered the conflict, and the dark malice of Claggart, and Billy's faltering speech, and the terrible earnestness of Captain Vere, and the wry world-weariness of the old Dansker — modes of being swirling and contending like gases in the primeval void, to coalesce into a particular universe, a configuration of events. Wasn't that enough? Not quite. What happens is important too. What do I have, then, after years of indulgence? A feel, a texture, an aura: the fragrance of Shakespeare, the crisp breeze of Tolstoy, the carnal stench of the great Euripides. Are they worth the investment of a life? Would my mind be more free without them?

In truth I have made some tentative steps toward freedom. Over the last ten years or so, I have managed not to finish certain books. With barely a twinge of conscience, I hurl down what bores me or doesn't give what I crave: ecstasy, transcendence, a thrill of mysterious connection. For, more than anything else, readers are thrill-seekers, though I don't read thrillers, not the kind sold under that label, anyway. They don't thrill; only language thrills.

I had put aside books before, naturally, but with guilt, sneaking them back to the shelves in the dark. It seemed a rudeness of the worst sort. A voice was attempting to speak to me and I refused to listen. A spiritual rudeness. Since childhood I had thought of reading as holy, and like all sacraments, it had acquired a stiff halo of duty. My cavalier throwing over a book midway may arise from the same general desacralization as does the notable increase in divorce, marriage also being a sacrament and, once entered upon, a duty. Every day joy and duty pull farther apart, like Siamese twins undergoing an excruciating but salutary operation: they were never meant to share a skin; they may look alike but their souls are different.

So, like recidivist marryers, I take up the new book in good faith, planning to accompany it, for better or for worse, till the last page us do part, but . . . it stops being fun. Other, more intriguing, books send out pheromones. There are after all so many delectable books in the world. Why linger with one that doesn't offer new delights, take me somewhere I've never been? I feel detached from the book on my lap much as the disaffected husband or wife feels detached from the body alongside and asks, why am I here, in this state of withness? In a marriage, one hopes it may be a transient feeling — there may be extenuating circumstances, although these lately do not seem to possess great force — but in the case of a book, why not be abandoned, and abandon?

This is a far cry from my idealism at age twenty, when I longed to read everything, simply because it was written, like adventurers who climb Mount Everest because it is there. Other sensationalists must sample everything edible or try every feasible sexual posture, however slimy or arduous, respectively. Thus do they assure themselves they have truly lived. No experience has passed them by, as if exhaustiveness were the measure of the good life.

Gradually I lost, or shed, the Mount Everest syndrome. Bookshelves still tease and tantalize, but like a woman with a divining rod, I know now where the water will be, I do not have to scrape earth and dig holes seeking, only there where the rod begins to tremble.

The unfinished or unread books languish on my shelves, some bought because friends said I must read them (but it was they who had to read them), or because the reviews throbbed with largesse of spirit (but it was the reviewer I loved, just as Priscilla loved John Alden or Roxane, Cyrano. I should have bought the reviewer's book). Others were just too gorgeously packaged to resist. Book jackets nowadays have become an art form, and browsing through a bookstore is a feast for the eyes.

In some cases the jacket turns out to be the best thing about the book. I am not one to snub beauty, wherever it turns up. Yet I have come to distrust book jackets calculated to prick desire like a Bloomingdale's window, as if you could wear what you read. The great French novels used to come in plain shiny yellow jackets, and the drab Modern Library uniforms hid the most lavish loot.

Once in a while I take my castoffs down and turn their pages for exercise, stroke them a bit. They have the slightly dusty, forlorn patina of people seldom held or loved, while their neighbors stand upright with self-esteem, for having been known, partaken of intimacies. I am regretful, but my heart is hardened.

I can face myself, abandoning even the most sanctified or stylish books, but there is forever the world to face, world without end. I envision a scenario: a group of writers sits around talking of the formative books, the great themes, let's say man grappling with nature, with death. Perhaps they are women writers, musing on men's compulsion to view everything in terms of struggle and mastery. One turns to me, saying, Well, for instance, *Moby Dick?*

I cannot lie about reading. A remnant of holiness still clings. It would be tantamount to a devout Catholic's claiming falsely to be in a state of grace. So I blush, confess I never finished it, and though they remain courteous, repressed shock and disapproval permeate the room (or could it be the women find me daring, the Emma Goldman of reading?).

I puzzled for years over how a friend, frantically busy at a publishing job, where manuscripts are thrust at you daily for overnight perusal, had read every book ever mentioned. Colossal erudition, I thought in my innocence, and speedy too. Till it struck me, as it might a child suddenly seeing through Santa Claus: it can't be. She lies. I wasn't filled with indignation, didn't even banish her from the ranks of the trustworthy. Simply: aha, so that's what's done, a helpful currency of social exchange like the white lie, and equally easy. You read reviews and jacket copy, and listen carefully. If you are reasonably *au courant*, who knows, you may even come up with critical judgments no less plausible or even valid than had you read the book. What has been lost, after all? Only the actual experience, the long slow being with the book, feeling the shape of the words, their roll and tumble in the ear.

Still, lying about reading feels too risky, as risky as saying you have seen God or drunk the milk of Paradise when you haven't — the kind of lie that might dilute the milk of Paradise should it ever be offered you.

Nor can I throw a book away. I have given many away and ripped a few in half, but as with warring nations, destruction shows regard: the enemy is a power to reckon with. Throwing a book out shows contempt for an effort of the spirit. Not that I haven't tried. Among some tossed-out books of my daughters which I rescued, to shelter until a foster home could be arranged, was one too awful to live. I returned it to the trash, resisting the urge to say a few parting words. All day long the thought of its mingling with chicken bones and olive pits nagged at me. Half a dozen times I removed it and replaced it, like an executioner with scruples about capital punishment. Finally I put it on a high shelf where I wouldn't have to see it. Life imprisonment. Someday my children, going through my effects, will say, "Why did she keep this wretched thing? She hated it." "Oh, you know what she was like. It was a book, after all."

To tell the truth, I had begun to think about reading before coming upon Mr. Cha. It was the spring of 1986, an uneasy time for me but a magnificent season for the New York Mets. As often happens with a new love or addiction, I didn't know I cared until it was too late. I had never followed baseball and felt safe from television, one of the devil's ploys to buy our souls. But alas we are never safe; in the midst of life we are in death, and so forth. My family watched the Mets. At first I would drift through the living room and glance, with faint contempt, at the screen. Gradually I would stand there for longer and longer spells, until I came to know the players by name and disposition and personal idiosyncrasies: how they spit and how they chewed, how they reacted to a failed at-bat — with impassivity or miming the ritual "darn-it" gestures — how their uniforms fit and which folds they tugged in moments of stress. The game itself I already knew in rudimentary form, having played punch ball on the summer evening streets of Brooklyn as the light fell behind the brick houses and the pink Spaldeen grew dimmer with each hopeful arc through the twilit air. All that remained was for the finer points to be explained to me. I was surprised and touched by the element of sacrifice, as in the sacrifice fly (the adjective evoking *esprit de corps* and a tenuous religiosity) and the bunt, a silly-looking play, several grown men converging to creep after a slowly and imperturbably rolling ball. I was impressed by the intricate comparative philosophy of relief pitching, and shocked by the logistics of stealing bases. This sounded illicit yet everyone took it for granted, like white-collar crime, with the most expert thieves held in high esteem like savvy Wall Street players. Then one evening — the turning point — I sat down, committing my body to the chair, my eyes to the screen, my soul to the national Oversoul.

I pretended an anthropological detachment. My quest was for the subtleties and symbolism — the tension of the 3–2 call, the heartbreak of men left stranded on base, the managers' far-seeing calculations recalling the projections of chess players (if he does this, I'll do that), the baffling streaks and slumps, and above all the mystifying signs. For at critical junctures, advisors sprinkled on the field or in the dugout would pat their chests and thighs and affect physical tics in a cabalistic language. Soon it was clear I wasn't as detached as I pretended. The fortunes of the Mets, as well as the fluctuations of each individual Met, had come to matter. It was partly proximity, the *sine qua non* of most love, and partly aesthetics. When giraffe-like Darryl Strawberry lazily unfurled an arm to allow a fly ball to nestle in his glove, I felt the elation I used to feel watching André Eglevsky of the New York City Ballet leap and stay aloft so long it seemed he had forgotten what he owed to gravity. Not unlike the elation I got from books.

I never watched an entire game, though. I hadn't the patience. I would enter late, around the fourth or fifth inning, when the atmosphere was already set — not that it couldn't change in an instant, that was part of the charm. I was like those drinkers who assure themselves they can stop any time they choose. I could start any time I chose. I was not compelled to scoot to my chair at the opening notes of the *Star-Spangled Banner* like a pitiful little iron filing within range of the magnet.

Night after astounding night became a season of protracted ecstasy. It was not just the winning but the beauty of the plays and the flowering of each distinct personality: modest Mookie Wilson's radiant amiability and knack of doing the right thing at the right moment, boyish Gary Carter's packaged public-relations grin, Howard Johnson's baffling lack of personality, absorbent like a potent black hole at the center of the team, Roger McDowell's inanity, Bob Ojeda's strong-jawed strength and the departures and returns of his mustache, Keith Hernandez's smoldering and handsome anger at the world, Len Dykstra's rooted insecurities packed together to form a dense and lethal weapon, Dwight Gooden's young inscrutability, reflecting the enigma of the team — arrogant or just ardent? All became crystallized.

Amidst the glory was an unease, a tingling of an inner layer of skin. I grudged the hours. I felt forced to watch against my will. Yet what was the trouble? Watching baseball is harmless, unless compulsion itself be considered blameworthy — but I am not that stern a moralist.

The games were depriving me of something. There it was.

The instant I identified the uneasy feeling as "missing," all came clear. Reading. Reading was the stable backdrop against which my life was played. It was what I used to do through long evenings. Never mornings — even to one so self-indulgent, it seems slightly sinful to wake up and immediately sit down with a book — and afternoons only now and then. In daylight I would pay what I owed the world. Reading was the reward, a solitary, obscure, nocturnal reward. It was what I got everything else (living) out of the way in order to do. Now the lack was taking its toll. I was having withdrawal symptoms.

I tried to give up baseball. I cut back, backslid, struggled the well-documented struggle. And then, abruptly, my efforts were needless. The burden fell from my shoulders as Zen masters say the load of snow falls from the bent bamboo branch at the moment of greatest tension, effortlessly. The Mets won the World Series and overnight, baseball was no more.

Had my struggle taken place eight years later, the much decried baseball strike would have snatched my burden from me in a more cruelly abrupt, un-Zen-like way. How many people suffered through nearly two years of baseball's defection, bitter and bereft, seeking other pastimes that would yield the same forgetfulness, the same sense of wandering companionably with like-minded dreamers through a green and grassy myth? They watched movies and game shows, they took up aerobics, they switched their allegiance to basketball or hockey (some may even have turned to reading). But, they reported, none of these felt quite the same.

I was never a true devotee, just on a brief vacation, or aberration. I doubt that I would have suffered much, but I shall never know. Anyway, by then the team I loved, the names and the personalities — or personas — attached to them were gone. The Mets, as far as I was concerned, were no longer the Mets. Over and over I have been puzzled by the ruthless trading of players and the players' own promiscuity. How can you still root for a team, I've asked true fans, when the members change every year? Over and over I've been told it's the team that grips a fan's affections, not its individual components. But the team is an abstraction, a uniform, a logo, a pair of colors. The players are what matter, just as you cannot substitute paraphrased chapters for *Pride and Prejudice*, say, or *The Golden Bowl*, telling the same story in different words, and call it the same book.

In any case, my swift and troubling affair with baseball ended painlessly. The dramatic victory of the Series over, I returned to reading, to my life. Or was it to a retreat from life, the void at the center, from which, the Zen masters also say, all being springs?

How are we to spend our lives, anyway? That is the real question. We read to seek the answer, and the search itself — the task of a lifetime — becomes the answer. Which brings Mr. Cha back to mind. He knows what to do with his life. He treasures his free mind, or that part of it that Shunryu Suzuki, in *Zen Mind, Beginner's Mind*, calls "big mind," as opposed to the small mind concerned with particular daily events:

> The mind which is always on your side is not just your mind,
> it is universal mind, always the same, not different from

another's mind. It is Zen mind. It is big, big mind. This mind is whatever you see. Your true mind is always with whatever you see. Although you do not know your own mind, it is there — at the very moment you see something, it is there. . . . True mind is watching mind. You cannot say, "This is my self, my small mind, or my limited mind, and that is big mind." That is limiting yourself, restricting your true mind, objectifying your mind. Bodhidharma said, "In order to see a fish you must watch the water." Actually when you see water you see the true fish.

But some of us must see the fish in order to see the water. The water may be too transparent to grasp without varieties of fish to show its texture.

A poet friend of mine, after heart surgery, was advised by a nurse to take up meditation to reduce stress. "You must empty your mind," she said. "I've spent my life filling it," he replied. "How can you expect me to empty it?" The argument is verbal. In Buddhist paradoxes, empty can mean full and full, empty, in relation to mind and universe. Either way, though, I keep worrying about those fish, flickering beautiful things of this world. A pity if they were to become only means to an end, to a serene mind.

In *The Ambassadors*, mild, restrained Strether is sent to Paris to extricate a young man from his passion, and instead falls prey to the same passion. In a whirlwind of exhilaration he exhorts everyone around him to live. "To live, to live!" Very heady. Though not so, apparently, to Henry Mills Alden of Harper's Publishers, who rejected Henry James's manuscript

when it was first presented: "The scenario is interesting," he
wrote in his report,

> but it does not promise a popular novel. The tissues of it are
> too subtly fine for general appreciation. It is subjective, fold
> within fold of a complex mental web, in which the reader is
> lost if his much-wearied attention falters. A good proportion
> of the characters are American, but the scene is chiefly in
> Paris. The story (in its mere plot) centres about an American
> youth in Paris, who has been captivated by a charming
> French woman (separated from her husband) and the criti-
> cal situations are developed in connection with the efforts
> of his friends and relatives to rescue him. The moral in the
> end is that he is better off in this captivity than in the condi-
> tions to which his friends would restore him.
>
> I do not advise acceptance. We ought to do better.

Luckily for us, the fine-tissued novel did eventually gain the
sanction of print and hard covers, between which "To live!" becomes the awakened Strether's motto, the Jamesian equivalent of a bumper sticker. Was I living, I wondered when I first
read it, or simply reading? Were books the world, or at least a
world? How could I "live" when there was so much to be read
that ten lives could not be enough? And what is it, anyway, this
"living"? Have I ever done it? If it is merely James's euphemism
for knowing passion, well, I pass. Reading is not a disabling af-
fliction. I have done what people do, my life makes a reasonable showing. Can I go back to my books now? For if "living"
means indulging the cravings, why then . . .

There was life before reading. Not until the sixteenth century were manuscripts even available, except to monks and
royalty. What could it have been like? There was life before
language too — grunts and grimaces, tears and laughter (yet
how much laughter, without language?), shrieks and groans
and commiseration; all of that is easy to imagine. But to have
language and no books? What to do after the corn is ground
and the water hauled and the butter churned? Keep your mind
free, as Mr. Cha suggests? Without stories to free the mind,
emptiness might be true emptiness, like Freud's proverbial cigar. Well, there were storytellers, the old woman sitting at the
fireside entrancing the family, or the troubadour chanting
verses near the fountain in the piazza while women walked
from the village oven with warm breads on boards balanced
on their shoulders. But that is a social experience. With books
there are no fellow listeners, no fleshly storyteller, none of the
exertions of fellowship.

Historians contrast the unity and coherence of the Middle
Ages with modern social fragmentation: among the hundreds
of causes for the change might be numbered the privatization
of stories — from a communal activity, listeners bound together by words that gathered them in and made their dreams
audible — to a solitary voice whispering in your ear.

Today, in an odd quirk of history, public readings once again
are enjoying a heyday, if not in the town square then in the
corner bookstore or library or art gallery, the café or the park.
Everyone, it seems, is writing something, prose or poetry, and
everyone wants to read it aloud. We wring our hands collec-
tively — and with good reason — over the impending death of

the book at the hands of electronics, over widespread illiteracy and semiliteracy, and yet plenty of people will come to hear others read. How this can be seems a paradox, but no doubt history could show even more wildly polarized trends flourishing side by side.

Still, today's audiences are not seeking quite the same thing as their ancient counterparts. The troubadours, the golden-tongued grandmothers and village schoolmasters were prized for the wonder of their stories. They were the only source of stories. Now listeners come, I suspect, not so much to hear as to see the storyteller, in a spirit of celebrating celebrity itself. A curious cultishness has come to surround the writer — I think of how Dickens and Wilde crossed the ocean and strode down the gangplank to the roar of cheering crowds — as if the stories and the writer were one and the same.

But you cannot see or touch a voice. That is what makes it mysterious and subtle and endlessly alluring. And without the voices of my youth, my ghostly familiars, how could I have become myself?

I READ at an early age, three and a half. The girl upstairs taught me. Late afternoons, we stood at the black-board in her hallway and she drew signs that were the same, but in another sensory costume, as the words that came from our lips. Once I grasped the principle of conversion, that airy puffs of voice could have a visual counterpart, the rest, what teachers call "breaking the code," was routine.

The world existed to be read and I read it. Diamond Crystal Kosher Coarse Salt on the cylindrical container my mother shook over simmering pots, and Reg. U.S. Pat. Off. on every box and can, had the rhythms of the pounding verses the bigger girls chanted out on the street, twirling their jump ropes. Before I knew who I was or what I might be, I became the prodigy, the "reader." When friends visited, my father would summon me and hand me the *New York Times*, his finger aimed at the lead story. "Read that." I read, though those signs had no meaning. Sometimes the guests refused to be convinced, suspecting I had been coached like the big winners on radio quiz shows. So my father would invite them to test me with any article on any page. No four-year-old could have memorized the entire paper. And while they marveled at my freakish achievement, which seemed to exist apart from my physical being, I could return to my paper dolls.

If my usefulness and value to my parents lay in this power to amaze, then I had to keep doing it. Reading was the ticket that entitled me to my place in the world. But in school there were other bright children. Soon everyone could read. My ticket was fraying, sadly devalued, and I felt something like the panic Samson must have felt, shorn. What can we do once we are ordinary? The choice of hair for Samson's strength is not as arbitrary or peculiar as I once thought. If your identity rests in special powers, you shiver without them, naked to the wind whipping at the back of your neck.

It was too late to fashion another ticket and besides, I didn't have the means: irresistible charm or beauty or athletic prowess or saintliness. Could I just be here, of no special use at all, simply by having been born? I envied my blithe peers who didn't seem to be paying any stiff admission fee. I still do. When I stand on a platform and speak, I envy the audience who need only listen. My father's ghost is at my shoulder, his gaze not on me but on the guests. With a swift jerk of the head he chuckles and says, Just get a load of this.

Because I read when I could still believe in magic, reading was magical, not merely breaking a code or translating one set of symbols into another. The idea of translatability was itself magical, and so it remains. Semiotics, before it became a formal branch of study, was the sleight-of-hand way of the world: signs and things, things and signs, layered, sometimes jumbled, partners in a dance of allusion.

But living amid so many words, I overestimated their power and breadth. The world does not turn on words alone; it only seems to if the eye and mind are saturated with them. I undervalued the other senses. I wrote of the disproportion in a story about my father, "The Two Portraits of Rembrandt," but it goes for me too.

He lived by the word. Pictures were a crude, provisional mode of representation and communication, happily supplanted by the advent of language. People who still looked at pictures for information were in a pre-verbal state, babies or Neanderthals. The *Daily News*, "New York's Picture Newspaper," was a publication designed for the illiterate. . . . Likewise, *Life* Magazine, which prided itself on its photography; he would not have it in the house. . . .

Maybe it was their limitation and finiteness that he dis-
liked about pictures. He loved what was bountiful and
boundless and hated anything mean and narrow. . . . Pictures were circumscribed by their frames. A house, a tree,
a cloud, added up to a landscape, and that was the end of
it. The space of pictures is inner space, but he didn't look
into, he looked at. Words, though, could go on forever, lin-
ear, one opening the door to a dozen others, each new one
nudging at another door, and so on to infinite mansions of
meditation. Nor was there any limit to what you could say;
words bred more words, spawned definition, comparison,
analogy. A picture is worth a thousand words, I was told in
school. Confucius. But to me, too, the value seemed quite
the other way around. And why not ten thousand, a hundred thousand? Give me a picture and I could provide vol-
umes. Meanings might be embedded in the picture, but
only words could release them and at the same time, at the
instant they were born and borne from the picture, seize
them, give them shape and specific gravity. Nothing was really possessed or really real until it was incarnate in words.
Show and Tell opened every school day, but I rarely cared to
show anything. You could show forever, but how could you
be sure the essence had been transmitted, without words?
Words contained the knowledge, words *were* the knowledge,
the logos, and words verified that the knowledge was there.

My father's scorn was so powerful that I never looked at a
picture — really looked — until I was in college. To satisfy a re-
quirement, I took a survey course in art history and spent three

class hours a week in the dark, being shown slides. The young instructor evidently found it natural and useful to brood in the dark over the intricacies of pictures; his devotion gradually dislodged my learned or inherited contempt. I saw that pictures, too, could be read, that everything in them was a sign, just as words and phrases were signs. The picture was its own kind of story, with each line and brush stroke, each color and placement of an object bearing the narrative along; they had been selected from an infinity of choices, put there on purpose, and they added up.

Why do you think the painter put those broken eggs right there? the teacher asked. What do they do to the space they occupy? To the space around them? Why the ruined castle in the background? Or the splotch of red up in the corner? Instinctively I had asked the same questions about words in books. My thoughts had shaped themselves aurally, through the sounds of the words. Meanwhile I had looked at paintings and photographs the way I looked at anything in my line of sight — a tree, a house, a traffic light — as if it were simply there: the given. Now I began to see, and to think through seeing. It dawned on me that a picture was something made, that the wonder of it, beyond any particular beauty or skill of execution, was that it existed at all, that it had overcome and overlaid blank nothingness, as words convert a blank page into the bearer of a story. (A house or a traffic light is made too, with its own felicities or failures of design, as I eventually came to see. As far as a tree, only God can make one, as Joyce Kilmer told us in the poem we were forced to memorize in grade school — how the boys cackled at "the earth's sweet loving breast." Everything in the world may be construed as a triumph over nothingness. Or better still, as a manifestation of Shunryu Suzuki's "big mind": "True mind is watching mind.")

Above all, there was the pure visual pleasure a picture could give, a pleasure beyond what might be read in it. This pleasure the instructor did not discuss; perhaps it was obvious to everyone but me. Yes, it must have been: after all, I never expected or needed my music history professor to point out that a passage was beautiful. I took that for granted. I heard it.

The pleasure of looking came slowly, and I have not yet learned it through and through. Possibly no sensory pleasure that we haven't felt at least dimly in childhood is ever thoroughly our own. (If we have not enjoyed our bodies as infants and children, for instance, can we appreciate eroticism as adults? Is such a deprivation possible?) Nowadays, looking at a picture, I am now and then speared by a sharp joy in the eyes, and I know this must be what art lovers perpetually feel: the pure ecstatic shudder of the retina, which is so rarely given to me. Even when it is, I must acknowledge that my tastes, still childlike, run to the "pretty." Color and design delight me (Matisse and Monet), and composition too (Cézanne and Michelangelo). Well, why on earth not? They ask no special acuity of the viewer. Of course these are sophisticated artists, and by conscious effort I have learned what makes them sophisticated, but what I enjoy about them is the primitive feeling of visual "rightness," as in a sonata's harmonious chord resolution. Too often I've turned away from paintings that are harsh, troubling, downright "ugly," or else pale and muted — all of them pictures that better eyes than mine perceive as excellent. And this shrinking from the difficult, the inharmonious, and the subtle is precisely what irks me in readers who complain that a book is "too depressing" or "too demanding," too long or complicated. No way to explain that a book's merit has nothing to do with its degree of good cheer, or that a "depressing" book can give exquisite pleasure. I suspect that to take a similar pleasure in "unpretty" paintings, I would have to have been born with different genes, or been taught at an early age to love the act of seeing.

Incidentally, living by the word, by organized series of words, which is narrative, is a handicap when it comes to operating modern electronic devices like telephone answering machines or VCRs (not to mention computers and the phantasmagoric reaches of E-mail). Such ineptness is not due, as laughing children suppose, to quaintness or premature senility. It is simply that readers are accustomed to receiving information in the narrative mode. A row of minimally labeled buttons means nothing if the nerve paths aren't trained for it. True, the machines come with instructions, but those hover near the borderline of language, closer to the pulsating fragments of rock and roll, a different semiotics entirely. The teenagers laugh at their parents, while it is we who should be laughing at them, except that the loss of language is a somber joke. When my younger daughter translates the manuals into narrative form I too can make the machines work: "Instructions for a happy VCR: Turn TV switch on. Turn VCR switch on. Watch little red button light up. Keep VCR on while doing all the rest of this. Little red button should stay lit." I feel the familiar comfort of language performing its original task. If those of us who live by language become superfluous in years to come, it will not be because of the advance of technology, but the loss of coherent discourse.

I⟊ started — my reading, that is — innocently enough, and then it infiltrated. It didn't replace living; it infused it, till the two became inextricable, like molecules of hydrogen and oxygen in a bead of water. To part them could take violent and possibly lethal means, a spiritual electrolysis.

I read whatever I found in the house. It was an age of sets, and several were stored in the bedroom I inherited when I was ten and my sister left to get married. Dickens in brown leather with a black horizontal stripe was cozy looking, but the Harvard Classics in black leather and gold trim were forbidding — especially Plutarch's *Lives* and Marcus Aurelius and the *Confessions* of Saint Augustine. I did manage to find one, though, volume 17, containing all the Grimm and Andersen fairy tales, which I practically licked off the page. They tasted bitter and pungent, like curries. The most bittersweet story, exotic yet familiar, was "The Little Mermaid," and rereading it today, I can easily see why. Like me, the "silent and thoughtful" mermaid lusted after the world. No matter how ravishing and secure the undersea realm she shared with her five loving sisters, the world way above lured her from her earliest years. She craved light, the great ball of the sun that beneath the water's surface was translated into a purple glow. And she craved people, in all their splendor: "Fonder and fonder she became of human beings, more and more she longed for their company. Their world seemed to her to be so much larger than her own."

Of course there were human beings in my world, but I imagined the ones beyond, in the great world I sensed was out there, to be more glittering and sunlit. The mermaid had to wait years until she was permitted to rise to the sea's surface and glimpse the wonders her older sisters described. "Oh, if only I were fifteen," she lamented — quite as I did, for I too had an older sister who got dressed up and went gallivanting.

In time the mermaid, as we all know, trades her fish's tail for earthly legs, in the hope of winning her beloved prince as well as an immortal soul. The world, though, is not without its price: in a supreme sacrifice, she must let the sea witch cut out her tongue and she loses her voice, "the most beautiful voice on earth or sea." As a child I loved irony — each new turn was a painful and delicious surprise. Here the ironies are tortuous: the mermaid becomes the prince's companion, but has no way to tell him it was she who saved his life in a shipwreck. Instead he loves the girl who found him on the beach, mistakenly believing her to be his rescuer. "Oh, if only he knew that I gave my voice away forever, in order to be with him!"

At seven years old I had no prince, and was even less exercised about having an immortal soul. What I did care about

was having a voice. I wouldn't have given mine up for anything, I thought, as if even then I sensed that it would become
a vocation, the means to a life. I agonized over the mermaid's
lost tongue. If only she could write! Yes, she could learn to read
and write, then give her prince a letter explaining everything,
untangling the knots that hold stories in place and smoothing
the way for a future. But there is nothing so mundane as reading and writing in fairy tales, and in the sad ones (as distinct
from the happily-ever-after ones) there is no future either.

The little mermaid, the story intimates, will have her soul
eventually, because she has suffered so much. But what good
is a soul without a voice to give it expression — sound and
words? I'm not even sure, now that I think of it, that the part
promising her a soul was in the Harvard Classics volume 17
version of Andersen's story. I may have encountered it only in
the unadulterated translation I just read, which does indeed
feel longer and sadder and infinitely more lyrical, and whose
introduction complains of the "distorted and mutilated" Andersen often presented to children, "with bits left out here and
there, and other bits — freely invented and quite out of tune
with the real story — put in at random." The simplest thing
would be to go to the shelf and check my old Harvard Classics
volume 17, but that I cannot do. It is mysteriously gone.

Not gone is the Little Leather Library, preserved in my dining room, looking, feeling, and smelling exactly the same as
when I was ten: several dozen books the size of a cigarette case
and bound in soft forest green, their crumbling pages the color
of weak tea. Rudyard Kipling, Shakespeare's sonnets, Ibsen's *A
Doll's House*, Conan Doyle, side by side, strange bedfellows,

sticking together damply, crackling when you pulled one volume out. Next to Oscar Wilde's "The Happy Prince," the sad-
dest story I knew, was the almost equally sad but unpoetic story
of *The Man without a Country*, by Edward Everett Hale. Here
too the hero loves his country and ends unappreciated, in ig-
nominy. Philip Nolan, no prince but a Navy officer, in a moment of rage denounces the United States, wishing never to
hear of it again. His words are taken literally. His punishment
is to live out his life aboard ship, never permitted to hear a word
about home. It was a fairy tale horror — those thoughtless
wishes! — in the Harvard Classics volume 17 come true: a
flaring impulse rashly given voice, a slip of the tongue really,
becomes destiny. Words are indelible, said the story. Watch
each one before it hits the air!

Alongside *The Man without a Country* were *Hiawatha* and
Carmen and *Alice in Wonderland*, "Pippa Passes" and *Sonnets
from the Portuguese*, those last not so strange bedfellows, and
strangest of all, *The Strange Case of Dr. Jekyll and Mr. Hyde*:
"'Is this Mr. Hyde a person of small stature?' he inquired. 'Particularly small and particularly wicked-looking, is what the
maid calls him,' said the officer." I was small too. Was that a
bad omen? *Tales from the Arabian Nights* flanked *Tales* by Poe
and *The Rubaiyat of Omar Khayyám*. I had barely begun life
when I was told how dispensable I was:

> And fear not lest Existence closing your
> Account, and mine, should know the like no more;
> The Eternal Saki from that Bowl has pour'd
> Millions of Bubbles like us, and will pour.

Another volume contained *A Message to Garcia*, which my mother spoke of with reverence. The author, Elbert Hubbard, a turn-of-the-century journalist and editor of a periodical called *The Philistine*, rightly calls it a "literary trifle" and describes how it was written in an hour, printed in the March 1899 issue, and to his creditable surprise sold in the millions. It was translated into "all written languages," with a copy given to every railroad employee and soldier in Russia and every government employee in Japan. Starting with the example of a dutiful messenger dispatched to Cuba by President McKinley during the Spanish-American war, the little homily extols the employee or underling who gets the job done, no questions asked. Who can fault diligence and efficiency in the performing of one's work? At eleven all I managed was a shrug for such unexciting virtues. But today the call for unquestioning obedience rings ominously. No accident that its context is military (were the Russian soldiers given Tolstoy too?). Had the reading public, in 1899, possessed the imagination to see where slavishness could lead, they might well have preferred the "slipshod assistance, foolish inattention, dowdy indifference, and half-hearted work" that Hubbard finds so offensive. A precursor of trickle-down economics as well, he sees too much sympathy wasted on the "'downtrodden denizens of the sweatshop'" and the "'homeless wanderer searching for honest employment'" (his skeptical quotation marks), and suggests it be redirected:

> Let us drop a tear, too, for the men who are striving to carry on a great enterprise, whose working hours are not limited

by the whistle, and whose hair is fast turning white through the struggle to hold in line . . . slipshod imbecility and the heartless ingratitude which, but for their enterprise, would be both hungry, and homeless.

With some streamlining of style and diction and an allusion to the cybernetical Third Wave, these lines could be part of a current conservative think-tank study. *Le plus ça change . . .*

To give righteous Hubbard his due, I should mention that his principles led him to found a community in East Aurora, New York, based loosely on notions of harmonious living and organic farming, and turning out finely crafted furniture; there he also established the Roycroft Press, whose print shop produced handcrafted books in the William Morris tradition. Hubbard met his end on the *Lusitania*, famous for being sunk by a German submarine in 1915, also doing its duty, according to its lights.

No shrug of indifference, only of bafflement, for "La Belle Dame sans Merci." I couldn't imagine what ailed the knight-at-arms, "alone and palely loitering." So he went with the fair lady to her "elfin grot," and when he woke she was gone. Why this outing should leave him drained and doomed was a mystery. Children accept magic; intractable passion is asking too much.

Equally mysterious was "The Lady of Shalott." *Why* was she confined to her island and forced to see the world only in a mirror, to weave webs with "colours gay" depicting scenes she could never be in? *Why* would she be destroyed if just once she followed her desire and looked directly at Camelot? *Why* does she inspire fear, what horrid curse could she spread, so that no one comes to save her or cares about her plight? Tennyson feels no more need to explain the "fairy" woman's imprisonment than Keats to explain his knight's languishing. But the knight is a thrall to love. The lady? Thrall to what? Some unspeakable curse. The poet delights in the utter arbitrariness of it, and his perverse delight is the power of the poem. As I pondered these perversities — it was a Sunday afternoon, I was about ten, hunched on my bed in confusion — my parents kept calling me. It was time to go visiting, and then, for my uncle the dentist and his wife never gave us more than tunafish salad, we would drive out toward the ocean, Rockaway, and stop for hot dogs (fried clams for my father). I went downstairs to be carried off and forgot the Lady of Shalott, as the world forgot her.

It may have been from that moment that I contracted a phobia for which there is no name, the fear of being interrupted. (It may also be why, as I grew up, I came to prefer reading late at night, when the intrusive world has gone to bed.) Sometimes at the peak of intoxicating pleasures, I am visited by a panic: the phone or doorbell will ring, someone will need me or demand that I do something. Of course I needn't answer or oblige, but that is beside the point. The spell will have been broken. In fact the spell has already been broken. The panic itself is the interruption. I have interrupted myself. Oddly enough, very often the phone does ring, just as paranoiacs can have enemies. Life is designed to thwart ecstasy; whether we do it for ourselves or something does it for us is a minor issue.

I envied my older sister her uninterruptability. While I looked up immediately from my book when my name was called, she had the uncanny ability not to hear. I would test her as she read. It was like addressing a stone, except that with a stone, if we are imaginative enough, we can infer some kind of response, albeit in stone language. My sister appeared to be present, but she was in the book. This is a great and useful gift. The stunned petitioner retreats, daunted by an invisible power that can drown out the world.

When questioned, my sister said that she really did not hear when she was spoken to. Years later I observed the same power in my older daughter. Did she too fail to hear? No, she said, of course she heard, she just didn't answer. And clearly it was not the same, in her mind, as out-and-out rudeness. Feeling herself elsewhere, she acted accordingly. Perhaps I have never been that absorbed, but I doubt it. What I lack is pure negative self-assertion. These two are oldest children in the family, quite secure about what is their due. Younger children may be so glad to be called upon at all that they respond indiscriminately, ears cocked for any meager chance to be legitimized.

My younger daughter hears when she is spoken to, but has yet another reading peculiarity. She reads with music playing. Apparently she absorbs both book and music; she remembered that Billy Budd's blow killed Claggart, while I had read the story in total silence. I regard this tableau — so symmetrical, hands, ears, and eyes plugged in — with no comment, since I know how it feels to have one's personal habits always scrutinized and challenged. It was the *modus vivendi* of my youth. But I am confused. For the words are a song entering the ear too, an intricate *recitative*, and how can anyone listen to two pieces of music at once?

The practice, by the way, of questioning or criticizing any aspect of a family member's behavior is not an undiluted evil. It shows attachment to each other's lives and the curiosity that marks a loving, engaged intelligence, though enemies of the nuclear family would claim it is the loving engagement that kills. I was impressed, at an impressionable age, by a friend's father who never made any direct personal comments (though as I came to know him I heard plenty of oblique ones). A remarkable freedom seemed to be proffered — nothing you said or did could raise his eyebrows. Of course he never praised anyone either. While such a leveling of affect may be useful in a Zen master with a student, I do not think in this case that it was part and parcel of a transcendent world view. After a while I would feel homesick for the overheated ambiance of my own family, where little went unnoticed. You could never doubt you had made an impact.

Besides being preternaturally engaged, my parents were people of the book. Not people who kept up with literary trends but who revered and trusted the civilizing influence of the written word (though my father could be skeptical of its truth). Like me, they never threw away a book. There were books stored in both bedrooms I occupied, first the small one and then the larger one I inherited when my sister got married, my brother succeeding to the small one, all of us like children advancing through the grades.

The books in the first bedroom were etched into my visual memory along with the design of the wallpaper and angles of the furniture, the shadow a chair cast on the rug and how it was reflected in the mirror: *Captain Horatio Hornblower* and *Hercules, My Shipmate* and *Down to the Sea in Ships* (why the pervasive nautical theme I shall never know) and *Stars Fell on Alabama,* which I soon learned was a song too — Billie Holiday sings it. Not until decades later, though, did I discover that *Stars Fell on Alabama* refers to an actual event, a spectacular meteor shower in the summer of 1833, which dazzled and maybe also terrified the spectators and which they interpreted as a portent of heaven knows what. I found this out on a two-week visit to Tuscaloosa, Alabama, a flat drowsy town with some magnificent old Victorian houses, the University of Alabama, and a hallowed football tradition. Toward the end of my stay, the university was preparing for its homecoming game, the grandest of the year. Stacks of wooden pallets were piled high as a three-story building on the campus quad — the builders had to use ladders — for the great Saturday night bonfire. People arrived in caravans of trailers and pick-up trucks and set up campsites on vacant lots near the campus; they barbecued over open grills at night, sitting on plastic chairs gazing up at the sky as if waiting for more stars to fall. Just outside of town, past the inevitable strip of malls, was an unprepossessing shacklike restaurant called Dreamland, a fitting name for a place where stars might fall at any moment, and it boasted the best ribs in the country. They arrived, thick and glistening, on huge platters with mounds of packaged white bread to sop up the gravy. Outside was a starry night. As I sucked on the bones I was transported back to my old bedroom with the mysteriously titled book on the shelf.

Stars Fell on Alabama was written by Carl Carmer, a northerner who came to Tuscaloosa in the 1930s to teach history at the university; he became entranced by the eeriness of the land and its legends ("a land with a spell on it — not a good spell, always"). His book is an odd compendium of folklore, anecdote, and local customs, with lists of superstitions, names of quilting patterns, and fiddlers' songs. I might well have enjoyed it had I thought to open it back when I was ten years old. I certainly never thought when I gazed at the title on the spine that someday I would find myself under the very sky from which stars fell a century and a half ago, eating a kind of barbecued ribs I never dreamed existed, even in Dreamland.

I didn't read those books on the shelf in my first bedroom, but staring for years at their luridly colored jackets, I penetrated them in another way. My conjectures of them are as vivid as the books I read and forgot. And their titles, in my mind, are the opaque emblems of an era, while *A Message to Garcia* is transparently emblematic.

I would occasionally be invited into my sister's room to help her memorize poems. She was already in college while I was barely in grade school. She started young, at fifteen, a fact of which my parents were very proud. It was the custom, for a number of years, to skip bright children through the grades as quickly as possible. Those who took the regulation time and finished high school at eighteen were regarded in my household as dullards. My sister's record was among the speediest, and neither my brother nor I would be able to surpass or even equal it since there was less skipping in our day. The poems were for her college English class — another, more worthy custom was learning by heart. I was honored to drill her, in the bedroom that would someday be mine. This was before my brother was born and before I ever dared dream I would have a brother, for my mother would come up with a child at widely spaced intervals as if it had just occurred to her. Only later did I learn she had suffered frequent miscarriages — we three were the tenacious ones.

I sat on my sister's bed with a couple of fat anthologies on my lap as she flitted about the room tossing her long chestnut hair and reciting, "I must go down to the seas again, to the lonely sea and sky, And all I ask is a tall ship and a star to steer her by," or, in her excellent clear diction, "Ah, distinctly I remember, it was in the bleak December, And each separate dying ember wrought its ghost upon the floor." Then she would go out in cars with soldiers, leaving me with Louis Untermeyer and the others on my lap. As I pored over their selections, she, in my visions, danced in the romantic arms of men in uniform.

My favorite among my sister's poems was Poe's "Annabel Lee." There are many decorative things for a child to love in "Annabel Lee," but beyond all particulars, it possessed a quiddity, the "whatness" Stephen Daedalus defines as Aquinas's *claritas* or radiance. "This supreme quality," Stephen says, "is felt by the artist when the esthetic image is first conceived in his imagination." And that instant when "the clear radiance of the esthetic image is apprehended luminously by the mind," he calls "the enchantment of the heart." I felt enchantment of

the heart on the receiving end, the reader's, when I first apprehended certain works, and I feel it, with some puzzlement,
today.

"It was many and many a year ago, In a kingdom by the sea,
That a maiden there lived whom you may know . . ." Whom I
might know! How incredible! I never knew any of the people
written about in books; I never knew anyone who wrote them.
Yet the very suggestion was a gleam of hope. Also, despite being included in the fat gray book and taught in college, this
poem was unmistakably written for children, with clippety-
clop rhythms and alliteration and predictable rhymes. Other
poems in the collection clearly proclaimed Adults Only, Children Keep Out, but this was *about* children. It said so plainly
enough. "*I* was a child and *she* was a child." Children were being taken seriously, in a poem granting, at last, their love life.
"But our love it was stronger by far than the love Of those who
were older than we — Of many far wiser than we —." The
lines that enchanted me most were, "Can ever dissever my soul
from the soul Of the beautiful Annabel Lee." It was those
"s" sounds, hissing defiance, mourning, passion, threat. Especially "ever dissever" — a palindrome for the ear.

That children could love passionately was not a phenome-
non adults took into account. But here the word "love" was
repeated over and over — six times in the first two stanzas —
as if the poet's mouth couldn't get its fill, insatiable for it. In
my family we rarely used that word to each other or about
each other, or about anyone else. When my mother spoke
of couples who were "keeping company" or getting engaged,

she would say, "Of course she likes him," or, "She seems to like him," never that they loved each other, far less that they could be "in love," a phrase that seemed to denote a silly, weak-minded condition, embarrassing to own up to, bordering on the irresponsible or disreputable, and certainly not to be bruited about. Romantic love, from what I could gather, was for far less decent and intelligent people than we, who should know better. At the same time I had the impression that we took love (serious, abiding love) so much for granted, dwelt so intimately with it, that it was beneath our dignity to mention it; it would be as superfluous and vulgar as people mentioning that they bathe daily or pay their bills. Love might even be too powerful or holy a word to use, just as we were not supposed to write the word "God" but "G-d" instead, which offended me aesthetically, a distraction in the flow of reading, besides calling attention to a figure already receiving more than adequate attention.

Later on I was surprised, in books and in life, to find love named explicitly: "But Father, I love him," or indulgently, "What could the poor girl do? She loved him," or soberly, "Are you sure you really love him?" or fatefully, "He took one look at her and fell in love." In other families, evidently, love was neither too holy nor too foolish to name. But there in the poem, "love" was all over the place: my sister was enunciating it in her clear voice and mellifluous diction, in the bedroom with the casement windows that would be mine when she left to get married (having, tacitly, fallen in love).

There were a number of words in "Annabel Lee" that I

didn't understand. I figured out from the context that "seraphs" were something like angels. "Coveted" soon became bitterly clear — I heard its echo farther on in "envying." "The angels, not half so happy in heaven, Went envying her and me." My sister explained "kinsmen." But, strangely, I didn't ask about the crucial word, "sepulchre," so oddly shaped and spelled. I couldn't acknowledge — didn't want to — that Annabel Lee's kinsmen put her in a tomb. A mere child with a slight chill? How could a draft kill anyone? Maybe she wasn't really dead, maybe her kinsmen just took her away because they didn't like the narrator — he wasn't as highborn as they were. Besides, how could angels kill out of envy? Angels were supposed to be good. To chart the precise degree of my comprehension and where it crossed with my ignorance is impossible. I have lost the child's ability to know and not know simultaneously, which is the most savory part of aesthetic pain, like the salt in tears.

I loved the outrageous ending — the narrator says he sleeps every night next to Annabel Lee's tomb — yet it made me uneasy. I took everything literally. I had often seen the sea — Brooklyn too is a kingdom by the sea — and even at five I knew what would happen if you buried someone in the wet sand at the water's edge. But no matter. The narrator is mad with grief, and madness makes all things feasible. I imagine the stories told to five-year-olds today, in the therapeutic era, feature narrators who diligently "work through" their losses to reach some emotional stability. With all the rampant conformity of my early years, eccentricity was still tolerated as a mode of being in itself, not a stage on the way to cure.

Above all, the poem was about loss, my perennially favorite theme. I sensed I had lost something too, though what it was I have yet to discover. Maybe I lost it when I learned to read, or learned to speak, or first opened my eyes: that fullness of being of the infant — empty yet full, the Buddhists' and Mr. Cha's paradox — before it begins to detach self from surroundings.

On some shelf or other in the small bedroom I found Eugene Field's "Little Boy Blue," a masterpiece among tearjerkers. If you don't cry at "Little Boy Blue" you have to laugh, and I am not quite ready to laugh. Along with "Annabel Lee," it gave enchantment of the heart and set a standard for all future reading. Or rather it wasn't the poems themselves that set the standard, but the strong emotions they aroused. *Lycidas* never wrenched me as "Little Boy Blue" did, which can hardly mean it is the lesser poem, but does mean something about the capacities of childhood and the powers of simplicity.

"Little Boy Blue" was satisfying to my ear, though it did not swarm and buzz with Poe's inner rhymes. It too had some fine new words: "stanch" and "moulds": "His musket moulds in his hands," an admirable line. And "trundle-bed," which sounded like something children in poems would sleep in. There were two odd, unfamiliar phrasings: "The soldier was passing fair," which I read as "passably" fair, fair enough; only years later did I realize "passing" meant, literally, "going beyond." And "Time was when the little toy dog was new," one of those locutions you seldom hear but grasp immediately (though hard to parse or justify to a non-native speaker). How compressed and forceful: "time was," irony laced into the syntax like threads of chocolate in a marble cake.

I must have been five or so when I read "Little Boy Blue,"
and I wondered, as did his bereft toys, what happened to him.
Where did he go, why did he never wake? I thought the poem
was a mystery (indeed there is an awful mystery at its heart), a
sort of detective story that didn't give enough clues, or else I
didn't get them. If I had suspected the truth, I would still have
been put off by the "angel song" that "awakened" him, for
"awaken" suggests life and action. The boy had awakened from
life into death, meaning we are only sleeping before the eter-
nal day. I could never have accepted that. So far as I could see,
he vanished into his sleep. For as with "Annabel Lee," that
children could die without warning was unthinkable.

I wasn't aware that two babies in our extended family, both
boys, had died not long before. They would have been my first
cousins, which was no inconsiderable bond: we were a large
and close family, seven pairs of aunts and uncles on my father's
side and five on my mother's, all of them constantly visited and
visiting with their two or three or four children, a huge array
of characters whose progress through life was an open book.
With so many near destinies to keep track of, the critical intelligence my parents brought to bear on the ongoing vicissitudes
of the families was positively literary.

On Saturday afternoons my mother and her three sisters
would gather around my grandmother's kitchen table to report and analyze the doings of their late adolescent daughters.
Since I was a good deal younger than most of my cousins, I got
to sit and listen while they were out providing us with material.
Some went to college, some worked, a few were idle; some had

boyfriends and some didn't. Where had they been and with whom and what had they said and worn? Here was the patient building up of character I was used to and enraptured by in novels, and so what I was really doing, as I sat silently drinking glasses of tea and cracking walnuts, was reading, without a tangible book.

The presiding spirit of the book, supplying context and narrative tone, was my small, august grandmother with her sky-blue eyes and smooth white-gold hair. In her youth the hair had been red, I had heard tell, and the vanished red had left behind the golden tinge. During the day she wore her hair in a neat bun at her neck, but early in the morning and at bedtime it was combed out, released in a long, thick coil down her back. I knew this because I had slept over a few times and caught a glimpse of her in her bathrobe, looking remarkably girlish with that mane of powerful hair. During the Saturday afternoon chronicling sessions she invariably wore an apron, and now and then circled the table to scrape the oilcloth clean of bits of walnut shells. She made swooping arcs with her knife; the sound of the dull blade against the oilcloth was portentous, like a Beethoven motif. Then she scraped the assembled crumbs and shells into her waiting palm at the edge, never dropping a crumb. Every now and then she would shoo her useful but unloved cat into the cold pantry beyond. On a cot in the corner sat her half-brother, who rarely spoke but was a fairly benign presence, more than a plant but less than a full participant. Now and then my grandmother would hand him a glass of tea or a piece of sponge cake. The sisters could say anything they liked in front of him because he was deaf.

During the Depression, I was told, the sisters, with their husbands and children, had each lived on separate floors of the old brownstone; later, as times improved, they moved one by one into places of their own. My own sister would tell me about growing up with a litter of cousins strewn on every floor, and I listened with envy, just as I listened to fables of far-gone eras. Our present house was small, neat, and ordinary, and I could imagine nothing remotely fabulous happening in it. Never, I was sure, would I experience anything as picturesque as the Depression.

The large kitchen where we gathered was at the end of a long, dark hallway and was joined to the dining room by a pair of swinging glass doors in which I watched my reflection swell and shrink as I played at opening and shutting them. Outside was a small front yard with a lone tree and a flight of fourteen stone steps leading to the second floor, but I never saw anyone climb them. Their use was for stoop-ball, which I spent hours playing with the children across the street. Ten points if you caught it on one bounce, twenty for a fly, and a hundred if it hit the edge of a step and ricocheted right back. Our other pastime was riding on the iron gate which swung around almost three hundred sixty degrees and had convenient places between the slats, big enough for a child's feet.

Besides the talk, the stoop, and the gate, the other great charm of the house was the icebox. My grandmother would hold open its waiting door as the iceman ran down the long dark hall with a great block of ice in his huge tongs, scattering a wake of sparkles. Sometimes he left another block on the sidewalk while he made his delivery and, along with the children from across the street, I would rub my hands down its sleek sides and watch it diminish under my touch. In summer we crowded around the ice truck hoping to draw in some of its chill. Slivers fell from the truck; we grabbed them up to roll around in our palms. When the truck drove off it left an arc of ice slivers in the street, glinting like spilled gems from a treasure chest, too soon leaving a mere puddle as a remnant of their glory.

One day, with as little warning as Little Boy Blue's disappearance, men came and took away the icebox. In its place they brought a shiny new refrigerator. All my aunts congratulated my grandmother on this long overdue step into the modern world, and she beamed proudly as she cleaned the inside with a rag, then loaded it with food. But what would become of the iceman and the ice truck? Never again to smooth down those cold blocks with hot hands, or come dashing downstairs only to be warned sharply from the kitchen, "Wait, the iceman! Let the iceman pass!" Later I learned there was a famous play called *The Iceman Cometh* and I yearned to see it, to recapture some of the lost glamor of that old icebox. When I finally got my wish, at the age of seventeen or so, what a letdown: nothing but a bunch of played-out drunks sitting around in a sleazy bar. No iceman or icebox at all. The title derived from a cheap joke that by the end became a macabre metaphor. So much for nostalgia.

I don't know whether the two babies who would have been my cousins died unaccountably, like Little Boy Blue, or caught a chill, like Annabel Lee. I didn't discover their brief passage until decades later, through words dropped here and there. Death was the untold story, grief not graced with words. No wonder I read. In books I found explicitly, flamboyantly, everything censored in life.

For I must have known, somewhere, about Little Boy Blue. Why else would I have wept at the image of the toys "stanchly" awaiting the child who will never come, their dignity a blend of loyalty and ignorance? My sympathy was all for them. The poem is skewed in that direction, making the boy a renegade and betrayer, and the toys abandoned victims. The skewing is what rescues it from being a maudlin set piece. To side with the toys, as we are led to do, is to avoid the danger of siding with the child. But our safety is a delusion; as the poem rights itself in the mind, we feel the aftershock. Even today it is startling that Little Boy Blue should vanish so suddenly. He didn't even have a chill. He fully expected to return the next morning from his dream voyage: "Now, don't you go till I come," he tells his toys, "And don't you make any noise!" But it is he who will never again make noise.

We realize we are mortal very early, as soon as we begin to put inkling and evidence together, and "Little Boy Blue" trades on that secret the way other works trade on sex or cruelty. Anything that nudges so temptingly at the forbidden, and offers the lures of sonority besides, can hold us hostage forever, just as the clever witches of fairy tales capture innocents by preying on their vulnerabilities.

.   .   .

The bookshelves were lined with real mysteries, not just metaphysical ones, and of these my favorites were Erle Stanley
Gardner's. Perry Mason, Hamilton Burger, Paul Drake, and
Della Street, that all-suffering secretary who I knew even then
was missing something, a self, were fleshed out in my imagination long before they became shadows on a television screen.
I read racy, hard-boiled *Ellery Queen's Mystery Magazine*,
which arrived every month, and I was astonished when my father casually mentioned that Uncle Dan, his brother, actually
knew Ellery Queen. (So what "Annabel Lee" suggested was
true: you *could* know the people in books, or behind them.)
What is more, Ellery Queen was not one person but two, neither bearing that distinctive name. They were not detectives at
all but partners in the writing business. I was shaken with wonder that this could be, and even more, that Uncle Dan could
know them, speak to them, and visit them in, wonder of wonders, an apartment in Manhattan. But if anyone would know
a writer (writers, in this case), it would inevitably be Uncle
Dan, a figure bathed in sophistication. He wore expensive
clothes and drove flashy cars and ate in fancy restaurants
where he appeared to know the waiters and liked to pay the
check, and was not married. He had started out married but
his wife died of a mysterious illness, and so, though a middle-
aged man, he actually took women out on dates, women we
occasionally met in the fancy restaurants. Their style matched
his, and while they were sometimes mothers too, widowed or
divorced, they were not like the mothers I knew, plump and
sage, who wore aprons and presided over the kitchen and pre-

figured what their daughters would become. I did not have it in me to become one of these aproned figures, or the other, sleeker kind either. Meanwhile I read, maybe hoping to find out if there was anything else to become.

Before I could become anything, though, there was the question of what I already was. A great unknown. I think I accepted, in a confused, half-conscious way, that I was whatever my parents described or defined me as being. They were, after all, my parents; they must know, mustn't they? And they were much given to describing and defining their three children. They observed accurately, then made the error of fitting their observations into a prefabricated design: for instance, I read a lot and did well in school, so I was "intellectual," or, even more formidably, "an intellectual." Intellectual was not a complimentary term. My father referred to two second cousins, both women, as "the intelligentsia," in tones dripping with scorn. I could never get him to say exactly what was wrong with them; when I asked, his sharp look suggested that I should know for myself, but on the few occasions I met them I had liked them — lively and talkative, with fuzzy hair and intriguing accents. They lived on their own and I could practically smell the fresh staunch independence blowing from their pores. He must have found them arrogant know-it-alls, too assertive. It was all very well for women to be assertive — my mother was not meek — as long as they kept their assertions to their realm of expertise, the domestic.

Still, the label was not appealing. I vaguely sensed that my qualities fit into some other mold, or — did I even guess? — maybe they would fit in no mold at all but shape a design of their own. In the midst of such confusions, perhaps at about eight or nine years old, I discovered a book that told me more about who I was than anything before or since. That was *A Little Princess*, by Frances Hodgson Burnett, and I read it over and over, as children do with special books. I still return to it every few years; it draws me, the way a certain piece of music or a certain landscape draws people back every so often. Each time it bestows on me, yet again, some crucial knowledge that is all too easy to lose, that the world seems bent on making us forget.

I was never consigned to a boarding-school attic like the heroine, Sara Crewe, or forced to be a household drudge, nor did I fall from wealth and luxury only to return to it. Though the delicious freedom of the very young child is a luxury, and the darkening years of conformity — which in my case began early, around the time I was consigned to perform from the *New York Times* — are a kind of drudgery.

So it was for me, anyway, and I imagine for other child dreamers as well. Occasionally when I mention *A Little Princess* I find someone who is startled into rapt recall, and we exchange a look of recognition. There is nothing to match the affinity of people who were defined and nourished by the same book, who shared a fantasy life. What we dreamed together, in whatever distant places we grew up, was of something amorphous — large, open, and exotic — something for which there was no room at home and even less in school. We groped for the knowledge *A Little Princess* confers, which is that we truly are what we feel ourselves to be, that we can trust our inner certainty regardless of how others perceive us or what they wish us to become. This truth comes to everyone eventually, one way or another (at least I hope so), but I was lucky to find it in a book.

"If I am a princess in rags and tatters, I can be a princess inside," Sara thinks. "It would be easy to be a princess if I were dressed in cloth of gold, but it is a great deal more a triumph to be one all the time when no one knows it." The key word is not "princess" — my fantasies did not run to cloth of gold — but "inside." I had suspected that the life within was every bit as real as the life without, but no one had ever before reassured me. Sara Crewe, heroic in her rags, demonstrated the fortitude and patience needed until my inner vision could find its way into the actual world.

When her friend, the slow-witted Ermengarde, is entranced by Sara's fantasies and whispers, "Oh, Sara. It is like a story," Sara replies, "It *is* a story . . . *Everything's* a story. You are a story — I am a story. Miss Minchin [the mean headmistress] is a story." Story within story, rippling to the far edges of the world. We can make up our own as we go along. How much better to make it up for ourselves than to let others make it up for us.

Besides validating the life of the imagination, Sara was a lesson in how to confront the awesome and frustrating power of the adult world. Sara is subjugated by the tyrannical Miss Minchin; I grew up in an ordinary family setting, insofar as any family setting is ordinary. Still, I chafed against the shackles of childhood. From as far back as I can remember, I wanted to live the way grown-ups live. The force of children's yearnings is every bit as great as that of adults, yet they are powerless. So they behave with defiance, willfulness, petulance — I did, anyway — all the modes of showing desire without the means to attain what is desired. Frances Hodgson Burnett, Sara's creator, knew this: she writes in her autobiography of how, even at three years old, she realized "the immense fact that people who were grown up could do what they chose, and that there was no appeal against their omnipotence."

Despite Sara's passionate rage against Miss Minchin's injustice, she knows it would be useless to protest. "Her heart grew proud and sore, but she never told anyone what she felt." I, on the contrary, was given to struggling and fretting aloud to no avail. I envied Sara's silence; I grasped its force; I wanted it. Such silence comes out of a keen sense of reality and of power. For the only way to oppose a greater power is with inner might.

> I don't answer very often. I never answer when I can help it. When people are insulting you, there is nothing so good for them as not to say a word — just to look at them and *think* . . . When you will not fly into a passion people know you are stronger than they are, because you are strong enough to hold in your rage. . . . There's nothing so strong as rage except what makes you hold it in — that's stronger.

I heard a great deal of rage — vocal and terrifying — when I was small; in that way my household was not what I could call ordinary. And I thought rage must be powerful. It was certainly loud. I have spent the rest of my life learning that loudness is not a show of strength, and that the spirit is kept alive by trust in the inner voice and by holding firmly to the unnamed thing that Sara found at age eleven: the stronger thing that makes you hold rage in.

Nowadays, when the exhaustive — and exhausting — expression of feelings is considered the mark of emotional health, Sara's reserve is plainly subversive. The patronizing labels it might be given leap readily to mind. No matter. Sara's behavior, then and now, revives older labels like honor and dignity (not to mention pride), which will outlast our faddish ones. Even Miss Minchin is unsettled by Sara's demeanor after being reduced to poverty and consigned to the cold attic:

> If she had cried and sobbed and seemed frightened, Miss Minchin might almost have had more patience with her. She was a woman who liked to domineer and feel her power, and as she looked at Sara's pale little steadfast face and heard her proud little voice, she quite felt as if her might was being set at naught.

Precisely: Miss Minchin's might *is* being set at naught by a will firmer than her own. Giving vent to every feeling may provide quick comfort, but true self-possession — keeping your own mind free, in the words of Mr. Cha himself, the Buddhist who set off these recollections — has more lasting rewards. As Sara knows, the power that must perpetually assert itself is no power at all. True power is confident and has no need of display.

I WAS often bored as a child, and would complain to my mother that I had nothing to do. Invariably, she suggested I sew something or read. I didn't like to sew; I had little interest in any of the housewifely arts, although I did enjoy watching my mother casually toss one ingredient after another into her heavy glass bowls or battered gray pots, never using a recipe, so that I imagined cooking to be a kind of God-given wizardry. The setting in which she worked her spells was thoroughly low-tech: she was an artist of the minimal, using only the humblest of tools. Whether she was ignorant of the usual implements or abjured them I cannot say, but she mashed potatoes with a large spoon, not the criss-crossed masher I saw in friends' kitchens, beat eggs with a fork and not a whisk, and peeled potatoes with a knife rather than the customary peeler. She squeezed oranges on a green glass squeezer — a shallow little bowl with a ribbed mountain in the center, rising to a point; it seemed to violate the orange half placed on top of it which then was rotated excruciatingly in small arcs. The juice gathered in the bowl, which had a spout for pouring right into the glass, using a small strainer if, like my brother and me, you didn't like the pulp. The fanciest thing our kitchen could boast was the waffle iron, a contraption I adored, with its neat double grid that received the avalanche of batter, then snapped shut and within minutes congealed it into beautiful, sweet-smelling Euclidian squares — a three-dimensional, edible crossword puzzle.

My very favorite tool among my mother's small supply was the meat grinder. A large, heavy gray metal device that suggested a medieval torture instrument, it screwed firmly onto the edge of the kitchen table. Its top end was a funnel, but more evocatively curvaceous than a cone, rather like a large open flower, maybe a heliotrope. Into this flower-face turned up to the artificial sun of the kitchen light, my mother stuffed chunks of beef or liver, onion quarters, hard-boiled eggs. She turned the handle in a broad circular motion and the victimized food came out transformed: eggs chopped, onion shredded. Most dramatically, meat emerged from the circular grid in long spaghetti-like strings, dripping into the waiting bowl. There was something magical about this metamorphosis taking place in the innards of the grinder, and metamorphosis — whether it was thoughts into words or meat into dripping strands — was what fascinated me. I would implore my mother to let me use the grinder and occasionally she did, watching closely to see that my fingers were well out of the open flower-funnel before I began my vigorous, sadistic swoops of the handle.

Still, this was the work of a few moments. I had no greater urge to putter in the kitchen alongside my mother. I didn't like doing anything much, really, perhaps because children were supposed to like doing certain things — puttering, sports, excursions, arts and crafts — and for me any pleasure was weakened once it was sanctioned, invested with respectability and obligation. What I liked was sitting on my bed and having a book happen to me. No one could manipulate or interfere with that.

It was during one of those grinding sessions in the kitchen that I complained of having nothing to do and my mother recommended *A Tale of Two Cities*. I took her advice. For weeks, probably months, I sat on my bed cross-legged, grinding my way through *A Tale of Two Cities*. It was difficult and tedious, especially at the beginning, but I was determined to read it because my mother had said Dickens was a great writer. Scattered amidst the tedium were magnificent passages like the reunion of Lucie and Dr. Manette, or the trial scene, or the wicked Evremonde's driving his carriage through the slums, which carried me through the boring stretches as a weekend trip with a lover carries a lonesome person through solitary months. I didn't hunt for the "good parts," though, as I did later with books hotly passed from hand to hand — *The Amboy Dukes, Never Love a Stranger* — whose plots were merely bridges to the moments when fingers began surreptitiously inching up thighs. I read every word of Dickens, in the belief that I could not properly appreciate the good parts unless I read the boring parts. Maybe this is true, and shows a precocious sense of the relation of figure and ground, or maybe, despite my rebellious passivity, I was caught in the overpowering moralism of the age: pleasure was a reward after suffering or "discipline," never gratis.

As it happened, I might have done well to sew when my mother suggested it, for I was about to be humbled for my disdain of the housewifely arts. In the midst of *A Tale of Two Cities* I entered sixth grade and found that the girls were required to sew aprons and caps in preparation for our junior high school cooking class the following year. The apron quickly became my albatross, though what misdeed it symbolized I didn't know — a sin of omission, no doubt.

The white shapes were mercifully cut out for us by the teacher, her only act of mercy. We were to sew a strip of red binding around the apron's perimeter in a neat running stitch, approximately six stitches to the inch, then turn the binding over and hem it around the whole perimeter. In addition, there was an enigmatic little pocket over one hip, too small for kitchen utensils, and anyway, cooks do not carry their tools slung phallically from their hips like handymen or telephone repairmen. Nevertheless the pocket was required and it too got the red binding, twice around, and had to be stitched to the apron. The cap was a triangular piece of white cotton to be worn bandanna style, also with red binding. This endeavor, with its ripping and repairing, was the work of the entire school year, for I could not do the binding to the teacher's satisfaction. She was an aesthete: "Yet if it does not seem a moment's thought, Our stitching and unstitching has been naught." We would not graduate or embark on junior high school, she warned, unless the aprons and caps were finished, and well finished, no sloppy edges or crooked stitches. I cannot remember doing anything else in school that year except watching one girl's phenomenal breasts grow. At home I wept and stormed and finally got it done with my mother's help. She was not a much better seamstress than I but she was more patient and did not have the weight of resistance cramping her fingers.

I suspected we would never use the aprons, that they were only a refined instance of the sadism the schools excelled in. I was wrong. There was a cooking class in junior high, a large room with eight or ten units of sink, stove, cabinet, and counter, and we did wear our aprons and caps as we cooked cocoa and grilled cheese sandwiches and spaghetti with a tomato and on-ion sauce. Whatever we cooked we had to eat, under the gaze of cheerful young Miss Sklar, who laughed at our mishaps, and her colleague, Miss Sherry. She was old, with a pinched face and steel-rimmed spectacles and white hair and a stiff rubber collar around her neck which I later learned was a therapeutic device, but since Miss Sherry had reportedly worn it from time immemorial I presumed it had symbolic import, maybe a form of self-discipline like a hair shirt. When Miss Sherry pre-sided, the cooking class had the austerity of a convent.

Still wearing our aprons and caps, we were promoted in the spring to The Apartment, four fully furnished rooms behind an ordinary classroom door, signaling the wonders that doors might conceal. Several times a week we cleaned The Apart-ment and cooked in its kitchen; again, under Miss Sherry's rigid stare, we ate what we cooked. The Apartment contained nothing so charming as the orange squeezer or the waffle iron or the meat grinder, but otherwise there was virtually every-thing an apartment needed, except bookshelves.

Meanwhile, at home, I was plodding through the two cities from the first word to the last, alternately hating and loving but ever willing myself to go on, while the light faded beyond the lovely black-bordered casement windows that looked out over a row of backyards. Those were the two halves of my life that year, A Tale of Two Cities and the apron. They were hair shirt, neck brace, discipline.

·   ·   ·

My parents were people of the magazine as well as the book: the daily mail — dropped through a slot in our front door — held treasures in brown wrappers. I liked the *Reader's Digest* best because of the jokes and anecdotes. Everything in it was short and pithy, numberless capsules of cheap optimism that lodged in my young brain and required painful dislodging later, like bits of shrapnel. I also read the *Saturday Evening Post, Esquire,* and several women's magazines, *Redbook, Cosmopolitan* (not today's sexy rag but a sedate guide to female behavior), *McCall's,* the *Ladies' Home Journal,* and *Good Housekeeping.* Each contained four or five stories, sometimes serialized, as well as a condensed novel. The stories were "women's fiction," that is, about family and love, and were an invaluable index to the world, or I should say to the prevailing middle-class fantasy of the world. I studied the monthly columns — "Can This Marriage Be Saved?" and "Tell Me, Doctor." The gray-haired doctor's kindly face (a photograph accompanied every column) bore an unearthly wisdom, and the tone of his readers' questions was correspondingly pious. The war, which uprooted so many comforting assumptions, paradoxically reaped an age of belief and submission. Perhaps it was simply exhaustion that made people love advice, rules, anything to relieve the burden of living in the raw.

The marriages, it seemed, could always be saved with a bit of patience and forbearance. I had little use for forbearance. I liked a good fight, and my judgments were at odds with those of tepid Dr. Popenoe. I wanted the harassed wife to throw her interfering mother-in-law out of the house, or get her snoring husband up from his armchair and over to the sink. I longed each month for a marriage that could not be saved, and I think this happened once or twice in the course of ten years. Probably the husband was an alcoholic or a compulsive gambler, or had even kissed another woman.

The *Reader's Digest* ran a condensed book each month, the prize at the end. I had no violent feelings, then, about condensation, so I enjoyed these without worrying over what was left out or in what relation the author now stood to her mangled work. For a while my favorite condensed book was Thor Heyerdahl's *Kon-Tiki*, about a perilous trip across the Pacific in a raft, but *Kon-Tiki* was soon outranked by a book even more charged with suspense, which to this day evokes the tenuousness of every mortal moment: *Miracle at Carville*, by Betty Martin, a true story set in a lepers' hospital in Louisiana. I have forgotten a good deal about the book but am loath to go back and check it out. I might laugh. Not at the lepers but at what was indiscriminately receptive in my young self.

The story, in my probably distorted memories, is narrated by a young woman — a wife and mother — found to have leprosy and sent to Carville, which has the feel of an adult boarding school or camp, a less lofty magic mountain where struggle and aspiration are distilled into purer form. Carville's guiding motif — religion, almost — is illness; salvation is measured by degrees of health.

The heroine enters the insular society of doctors, nurses, fellow patients, and routines, all described in enormous and, to me, fascinating detail. Life at Carville is structured around the monthly blood tests. Positive means despair, negative means hope until the following month. A patient needs twelve consecutive negative tests to be declared cured and return to the world outside. The book too is structured around the test results, with the tension of a poker game or a tied ball game, where each moment promises a new future or prolongs the agonizing present. Time and again our heroine has four or five or six negatives, dares to dream, then draws a positive and must start all over. I read with every cell alert, curled up tight on my bed, choking with anticipation, hoping, despairing, marshaling new hope out of despair: the leper, *c'est moi*. Would we ever achieve the impossible twelve negatives and leave Carville? The constant temperature takings of *The Magic Mountain* are bland compared to Carville's ups and downs.

Then there is the love interest. The heroine's husband visits at intervals, but inevitably some estrangement creeps in. She inhabits an alien world with new premises and uncertain prospects. The very word "leprosy" is a turn-off. At a time when ignorance about the disease engendered panic, who could love a leper if not another leper? Yes, a man leper waits in the wings. They fall in love . . . Should they stay with their spouses who understand nothing of the critical experience of their lives, or start anew together? Even I, with all my experience of "Can This Marriage Be Saved?" hadn't the usual prompt solution. I think that after much agonizing the pair decides to stay together. And then the beauty of the structure is made manifest. Just as you expect the easing of a dénouement, the tension thickens. The twelve tests balk the lovers, as in a fairy tale or myth. He's almost made it, and she fails and has to begin again. She is practically cured, and his next test is positive. Relentless frustration. Years go by, maybe longer than Jacob labored for

Rachel. (Are they sleeping together? I hope so. It didn't occur to me to ask; I was barely eleven.)

I never forgot *Miracle at Carville*, but for a long time I didn't think about it. And then I lived in Hawaii for several months and visited the small island of Molokai. The Lonely Island, it was once called, and with good reason. Molokai was home to the former leper colony on the Kalaupapa Peninsula, a place notorious for its wretchedness and deprivation. In the mid-nineteenth century, Hawaii endured an epidemic of Hansen's disease. In the grip of ignorance, fear, and heartlessness, authorities resolved to isolate its victims on a two-mile strip of peninsula bounded on one side by the sea and by virtually un-crossable mountains on the other. Starting in 1866, there the sick were ferried with barely the means for sustenance, and there they remained to fend for themselves. Without social structures or organization, the sole support came from those family members who accompanied and nursed their loved ones.

Ironically, the place of exile was one of the most beautiful sites in the world, the kind of white beach and craggy moun-tain setting that today would be snapped up by developers for tourist resorts: Eden as a setting for *Lord of the Flies*, only its residents were not plucky British schoolboys but sick and abandoned adults.

In 1873 things began to change at Kalaupapa with the arrival of Father Damien, a Belgian priest who voluntarily took on the task of ministering to the sick and shaping a humane society out of chaos, pain, and disarray. Conditions were such that Fa-ther Damien spent his early days in Kalaupapa living under a

tree. He worked at digging graves, nursing the sick, and building shelters, until bit by bit the colony was transformed into a
community and the lives of its exiles redeemed. Damien was
regarded as a living saint and others came to join his efforts. He
contracted leprosy himself, died in 1889, and is still revered.

Today only a small number of people remain in the neat village on Kalaupapa. Now that the stigma of Hansen's disease
has abated they are free to return home, but they do not choose
to. They take pride in what was once a place of shame. The
peninsula can be reached only by plane or mule or a hike down
the mountains, and guided tours are offered. I didn't make the
trip; the idea of being a tourist in this former hell with the features of paradise somehow didn't sit well with me. I stood on
the Kalaupapa Overlook sixteen hundred feet above and
gazed down the steep mountain at the strip of scalloped beach.
It was a misty day. I was so high up, or it was so far down, that
banks of clouds separated us. For minutes at a time I could see
nothing but cloud, until suddenly the clouds would part to reveal the blue and white glory below, dotted with small buildings and palm trees. Then the mist quickly gathered anew and
within seconds I was isolated on the mountain — I could forget there was anything below. Just so the lepers must have been
forgotten, behind their barrier of mountain and mist. An instant later, when the clouds broke again, all was clear and serene. Pain appeared to have left no trace on the landscape, or
perhaps the special beauty of that pristine beach was the re-
demptive calm of pain visited and eased by love.

As for *Miracle at Carville*, seminal book of my youth, I can't
vouch for its outcome, but given the title I suppose the lovers

eventually passed the tests and lived happily ever after. Does the long reach of its influence lead me to invent torturous plots, suffering and relief in maddening alternation? Not at all. Next to *Miracle at Carville* my own novels are uneventful. I wish this were otherwise, but it does not seem within my control. I was surprised to hear a writer once say she wrote the sort of books she wanted to read, since no one else was writing them. Many people, most of them dead, have written the sorts of books I want to read. But not me. What we love to read is not necessarily what we write. The great Italian writer Natalia Ginzburg, who in her early years translated Proust, has described her longing to write lush, allusive prose entwining the complexities of soul and universe into every helical sentence. When she set pen to paper, what appeared was terse and straight as a bone.

But the tests, those twelve tests. They were what gripped me so tight, because my childhood was fenced at every turn with tests — from performing the *New York Times* to attending school, where understanding was quantified by tests, a world of measurements light-years from the way things felt inside. I tangled my insides trying to shape them to the world of quantification, quite like the leper who, however well she felt, however much in love she was, got tied in knots every month, her inner truth twisted by numbers popping out of a test tube and labeled, unaccountably, with her name.

My parents were people of the book: my mother read family sagas, historical romances, popular fiction by the current household names — Anya Seton, Faith Baldwin, Rumer Godden, Taylor Caldwell. My father read mysteries and, like many men, was in thrall to the *New York Times*. The relation between these pale loiterers and their *belle dame sans merci* is visceral, more potent than any mere sexual or emotional connection, and would require a Keats to do it justice. Some can loiter for fifteen minutes or more on a single page. An observant woman once informed me, "Don't you know? They're not really reading. It's their way of daydreaming, but they have to have the paper in front of them to justify it."

After the *Times* and the mysteries, my father liked books on political and historical topics: biographies of the presidents, Theodore White on the campaigns, William Shirer on the Third Reich. He was always interested in a new book on Roosevelt. He read as I do, slowly, absorbedly, the book at arm's length from his eyes, but as I cannot do, he read lying down, stretched diagonally on the bed, stockinged feet crossed. His right hand, which held a cigar, was behind his head, the right elbow sticking out at a sharp angle. His cigar of choice was likely to be a Corona Corona, in those days when Havana cigars were readily available, and I might even have gotten it for him. For when I was quite young he would occasionally summon me with the special charm of people about to ask a favor, hand me a few coins, and ask if I would run out to the candy store to buy him a cigar. This five-minute trip entailed crossing an avenue that at the time seemed broad and perilous, and which my mother did not allow me to cross alone until I was seven. I was proud of the privilege. I felt very grown up pocketing the coins and setting out on my mission, and I liked partaking of the wider world by abetting such an adult pleasure. I liked it even better if, as often happened, my father was relaxing on the front porch with a friend when he made his request, for then I could show off my speed and efficiency as I returned promptly, cigar in hand. He would always reward me with the gold-embossed paper ring adorning the cigar, which I liked to wear until it broke. This little errand was our joint performance, and it felt pleasant and fitting that I should oblige him. It was a far more reasonable request of a child, it seemed to me, than performing from the *New York Times* for his assembled guests. If he could read this he would be startled to know how bitterly I resented showing my reading prowess, just as I am startled myself, as I write of it.

Anyway, when he read he would lie on the bed with the cigar in his right hand burning down. His left arm was extended, the hand supporting the book from the bottom and turning its pages at the lower spine with a right-to-left flick of the thumb. He was still in his business clothes, white shirt unbuttoned at the neck and tie either hanging askew or removed, for he did not change into casual clothes when he came home from work. He had very few casual clothes, shorts for the summer and a few sport shirts he paraded around in on rare occasions, looking jauntily pleased with himself but slightly awkward too, seeking approval. He dressed in the morning and undressed when he went to bed and that was it, and he hated our walking around in pajamas or bathrobe once the day had officially begun. Or rather it was the dressing that made the day official — without our wearing the proper clothes, the day could not take hold, was tentative, amorphous, unpredictable, and he needed to have the day official and under control as soon as possible. When I lounged around in a robe on weekends, his look of distaste conveyed that my dishevelment was morally inadequate. To this day I have trouble walking around in a bathrobe past eleven in the morning, even though I am in my own house and he is dead. I feel unprepared for what life might require of me.

He could read in that position for a couple of hours so I guess he found it comfortable enough, and then he would fall asleep, his glasses slipping awry, the book coming to rest on his leg, the right hand still behind his head with the dead cigar between two fingers. I fall asleep reading too, and the last sentences filter into my dreams, where I continue writing the book. After spending several late evenings reading Ved Mehta's biographies of his parents, *Daddyji* and *Mamaji*, in dreams I invented long passages about Indian marriage rituals and domestic life, spinning off from the facts. I picture my father in his habitual pose whenever I see new books he would have taken pleasure in, about Entebbe or Watergate or the assassination of Kennedy, biographies of Johnson or Truman, books about the Vietnam War and PACs and oil conglomerates and the misdeeds of Congressmen. Sometimes I feel a funny urge to read them for him.

As much as my father approved of reading, he objected to my habit of reading at the table. He wanted civilized dinners with the family gathered round in conversation. Reading at the table is uncivil, yet few acts are so completely satisfying. The two infusions, food and words, intermingle. The rhythms of chewing and swallowing join with the rhythms of sentences in a fantastic duet where the ear can barely separate the melodic strands. Parallel lines meet: food and story converge in mouthfuls of narrative, and the misleading duality of flesh and spirit is overcome. I will never be able to dissociate *Heidi*, a book I read again and again, from the accompaniment of lamb chops and mashed potatoes — a far cry from the fresh goat's milk her grandfather was forever pressing on her — just as some people cannot dissociate sex from marijuana or baseball games from hot dogs.

I would get to the last page and flip back to the first, unwilling to let it go, have it end. It didn't matter that I knew what was going to happen. I never read for the story, only for the taste. I can't say how many times I read *Heidi* before I moved on to *Heidi Grows Up* and *Heidi and Peter*, each one more attenuated, like succeeding cups of tea from the same tea bag (and indeed I recently learned that the sequels to *Heidi* were written by the French translator, Charles Tritten). For some reason, maybe the alien sound of the name, I assumed the author of *Heidi*, Johanna Spyri, was a man, even though I knew women wrote books: there was Louisa May Alcott, whose entire sunny *oeuvre* I had read (only lately, with serious studies of women's writing, have her darker works been reissued). When I had had my fill of *Heidi* I found a new book by this remarkable "man": *Cornelli*, addressed directly to me. How could "he" have known?

Cornelli is another displaced Swiss girl. Her mother has died, and to ease, or, more accurately, correct her inconsolable grief, her father sends her to live with a wholesome mountain family, where her gloom makes a sharp contrast. The mother of the family tells Cornelli that if she persists in frowning she will grow two little horns between her eyes, like the ubiquitous goats. Cornelli was as literal minded as I. We didn't realize that the horns were the bumps between the eyes on a perpetually furrowed brow. Since she cannot stop frowning, Cornelli takes to wearing her hair hanging over her eyes to mask the horns. Everyone in the happy family mocks her messy hair and tries to get her to comb it back, but she is horrified that the horns, sign of her grief, will show, that suffering will have deformed her into an animal. Meanwhile her pain has been forcibly shifted from the loss of her mother to her dehumanized state. She is made ashamed of feeling as she does, being what she is. Naturally I didn't see all this when I read it. I worried endlessly and indignantly over Cornelli. She was entitled to her horns, I felt, entitled to sulk and shield herself with her hair, just as I felt entitled to the sulks I had to fight for.

At last someone, probably the well-meaning mother, breaks through the veils of misunderstanding to the source of Cornelli's trouble and explains that she will not grow horns, it was only a figure of speech. Relieved, reached, Cornelli allows her hair to be combed back. The furrows in her brow smooth out, her mourning recedes, and she can regard the world without a protective mask. If I could uncover why I cherished this book so deeply, what exactly I was grieving for and why I clung to the grief, it would be a great unmasking.

There were some books I wanted to possess even more intimately than by reading. I would clutch them to my heart and long to break through the chest wall, making them part of me, or else press my body into them, to burrow between the pages. When I was eight I felt this passion — androgynous, seeking both to penetrate and encompass — for *Little Women*, which I had read several times. Frustrated, I began copying it into a notebook. With the first few pages I felt delirious, but the project quickly palled. It was just words, the same words I had read over and over; writing them down did not bring me into closer possession. Only later did I understand that I wanted to have written *Little Women*, conceived and gestated it and felt its words delivered from my own pen. But that could never be, unless I did as Borges's Pierre Menard, who undertakes to rewrite *Don Quixote*, but in order to do so must reinvent in himself the sensibility of a seventeenth-century Spaniard. I did not want to feel and think like Louisa May Alcott, however, or even to know more about her. I wanted to write my version of *Little Women*, what Louisa May Alcott would write were she in my place, or if I were she, yet living my life. But the notion of "if I were she" or "if she were I" boggles the mind, an absurdity even grammatically. (If I were she I would no longer be I.) When we yearn to be someone else, what part of the "I" do we imagine detached and transplanted? The self has no discrete movable parts.

Since then, from time to time I have felt the urge to copy certain books: *The Death of Ivan Ilyich* and *Middlemarch* and Margaret Drabble's early novel, *The Millstone*; stories by William Maxwell and Pavese and Natalia Ginzburg (I have translated some of hers, a more useful way of possessing); and Calvino's *If on a Winter's Night a Traveler*, a paean to the act of reading in all its richness, infused with tenderness to readers, a novel whose narrative thread is drawn by the needle of reading.

I don't copy them. I do recognize them as books I want to have written, which, given enough talent and ingenuity and time, I might have written. I was groping toward them and might have reached them in a few centuries, but others reached them first. And it appears that the critical thing these others were able to do was identify and localize a subject that for me remained undefined and elusive — until I read their books and saw it clear and elegant. In that light, writing seems less a craft than a quality of mind and discernment, a rarefied focusing. Or sometimes the other writers have lit on the perfect form, which obviates any struggling for subject — Proust's ruminating novel or Herbert Morris's meditative poems like an intimate conversation, both unabashed about their length, or, in the short department, Robert Walser's idiosyncratic essays like messages found in bottles, comically wry and desperate. Then I think, Had I only known you could do it that way . . . and writing seems a function of inventiveness and nerve. In any case, the books I have wanted to write brood about what I brood about, and they move in uncannily familiar rhythms. Reading them, I feel caught out. Some stranger, like the author of *Cornelli*, has preempted my secrets. I am disarmed, but less alone.

There are equally fine books that, much as I admire them, I would not have wanted to write, indeed have been relieved I didn't need to write: *Madame Bovary, The Idiot, Mrs. Dalloway, Dubliners*. Too difficult, too impossible to sustain such crushing moods and temperaments. But I am judging by my own powers of endurance. Again, were I those writers, I could and would be they; the issue evaporates into tautology.

Ticklish questions of identity inform another treasured book, which few people seem to know: *Martin Pippin in the Daisy Field*, by the prolific British writer of children's books, Eleanor Farjeon. The French surrealists would have approved of it — arbitrary, dreamy, mystifying, leaning heavily on the *non sequitur* and the extravagant. Martin Pippin, part rural Prospero, part Puck, is in the daisy field with six little girls — Sally, Sophie, Selina, Sue, Sylvia, and Stella — who insist he tell them each a bedtime story, which he does. Meanwhile, in interludes, a riddle of identity is worked out. Martin Pippin must guess who the girls' parents are, with nothing to go on but six pairs of names and a handful of character traits. The girls tease and confound him by mixing up names and clues, cavorting with the mysteries of identity; the narrative often sounds like Virginia Woolf rewriting *The Waves* for young readers. In the end the girls, and their fathers and mothers, are figments of Martin's bucolic dreams, projections of the child he may someday have — for he has gotten married that afternoon, it turns out.

Martin Pippin embodies a name game of the highest order, playing with the protean nature of names, which can empty or swell like a bellows according to what we know or imagine of the reality behind the name. It is the sort of game Proust plays with the names of towns in Normandy and Brittany, or with Florence and Venice, whose syllables, he finds, not only evoke but contain, in tiny quanta of impressions, the light, the smells, the flavors and texture of the place.

Our sense of a name and the people who bear it may depend on someone we knew in childhood, a Katharine, perhaps, prim and chirping and knock-kneed, so that we expect every Katharine thereafter to wear Peter Pan collars and be a soprano. If we find a variant, Katharine Hepburn, for instance, we must laboriously detach the original qualities from the name and graft on new ones. And still the name is never entirely free. No matter how many variants, it keeps vestigial traits of its original. So, with primitive attachments, parents name their children Richard (the Lion-Hearted) or Arthur or Helen, but rarely Cassandra — few want a truthteller. Many such names are chosen for their singular destinies — kingly Davids and wise Samuels — while others are shunned: who names a child Cain or Goliath or Judas? And naming boys after their fathers is not only a bid for literal immortality but a wish that the boy carry on the virtues of his father, be his father. Among Jews that particular *hubris* does not operate. Children are named after the dead, so that the dead won't be lonesome but will, as my mother used to say, "have someone." In the end it is the names, not the people, that are immortal, absorbing the history of everyone who has borne them. The delicate infant, innocent of the density of her name, unwittingly adds her bit of character and fate.

Besides the intrigue of names, Martin Pippin's game hinted at the enigmas of heredity, which children love to ponder. They dazzle themselves with fantasies of being adopted, and the adopted ones dream of finding their "real" parents and grasping the ineffable. Why are we who we are? I would ask, sitting on my bed under the casement windows. I imagined springing from different, idealized parents, but then I would not have been myself. Had I been conceived on another day or in another room, even, I might have been someone else.

How energetically we resist becoming updated versions of our parents. Of course we cannot create new genes, but with effort, we believe, we can grow new traits and modes of life: self-generated mutations. Yet when we do manage to create ourselves anew, isn't there always a suspicion that the new identity fits over the old like a second skin, at times itchy or uncomfortably tight, not quite covering the most vulnerable patches? Caught unawares — awakened from sleep or weakened by illness or stress — we find ourselves behaving exactly as our parents did, the genes asserting themselves through the flimsy new skins, their power unabated.

My favorite of Martin Pippin's stories was "Elsie Piddock Skips in Her Sleep," set in the village of Glynde, under Caburn Hill, where the children "lived mostly on bread and butter, because their mothers were too poor to buy cake." When she is three years old Elsie Piddock hears the bigger girls outside skipping rope to the rhyme,

Andy
Spandy
Sugardy
Candy
French

Almond

ROCK!

Breadandbutterforyoursupper'sallyourmother'sGOT!

She starts skipping at that early age — just the age I learned to read — and her fame spreads throughout the country, for she is a born skipper. The fairies soon hear of her, and she becomes the protégé of their skipping master, Andy-Spandy. Every month at the new moon, fast asleep, she joins their mid-night skipfests on Caburn Hill, where Andy-Spandy teaches her the magic skips. She can skip high and low, fast and slow, she can skip over the moon or to the earth's core; she can skip through a keyhole and land on a blade of grass as lightly as a drop of dew.

Andy-Spandy is the source of art, imagination given shape; as his apprentice, Elsie Piddock follows all he says without question. When her training is done he licks the wooden han-dles of her rope and they become Sugar Candy and French Almond Rock. "You shall therefore suck sweet all your life," he tells her, and though I was too young to know the links be-tween Art and Eros, I must have known somewhere, as I knew about death, that they were holographic, sliding into each other depending on the slant of light and the tilt of the mind contemplating them. Elsie Piddock can return at any time to the tool of her craft, touched by the lips of imagination, to find solace and nourishment. After a lifetime of skipping, "when times were hard, and they often were, she sat by the hearth with her dry crust and no butter, and sucked the Sugar Candy that Andy-Spandy had given her for life."

Years later, when Elsie Piddock has become a legend, a great Lord, a prototypical industrial magnate, decides to fence off the skipping ground at Caburn Hill and build smoky factories. The village girls, their mothers and grandmothers who grew up skipping there, are heartbroken. But what good are feeling and tradition against the march of industry? Suddenly an old woman appears, tiny as a child, and bargains with the Lord for one last moonlight skip. Only when everyone from lithe girl to achy crone has skipped till she stumbles, the Lord agrees, will he start building his fence. He waits impatiently. Just as it seems over, the tiny old woman reappears: Elsie Piddock, one hundred nine years old. "When I skip my last skip," she announces, "you shall lay your first brick." But she never does skip her last skip. She goes on forever. She is skipping even now. Thanks to her moonlight dreaming sojourns among the fairies, she has become immortal. Her art will outlast the greed of entrepreneurs and the machinations of city councils and the carelessness of parliamentary decrees. It will last as long as the hill she skips on and the moonlight she skips under.

Here was a story for me to lean on, and live on. It said that the things I loved were not foolish or frivolous. Elsie Piddock may have been dreaming when she apprenticed herself to Andy-Spandy, but in the end art is not only dreaming but action.

MAYBE that early impulse to possess the books I loved by copying them is what moviemakers feel. Ever more avidly, they have been dusting off old books like costumes found in the attic, to rip them apart at the seams and redesign them for their screens. I'm aware that money is a powerful motive here, but I like to think love plays a part as well. Certainly love, of the reverential kind, inspired the "Masterpiece Theatre" television series, which brought us the likes of Henry James and Jane Austen in living color, with fatherly Alastair Cooke as mediator: he would explain the subtle points and refresh our memories week to week, like the little summaries heading each serialized novel installment in the women's magazines. "Masterpiece Theatre" had its charms — Purcell's heraldic trumpet music summoning us to the TV set, the camera panning over those dignified leather bindings, and the Sunday night time slot, which gave the sense of starting the week on a virtuous note — and yet the aura of pomp made for distance. Great books are best enjoyed as intimates, not decked out in regal trappings. Did *The Golden Bowl* find more readers as a result of its TV excursion? Or did relieved viewers heave a sigh: Well, now I know what that's all about, I don't have to read it. Is it "better" to have seen the televised version than never to have encountered James at all? Assuming, that is, that watching television can in any sense be an encounter with James, the writer.

One way or another, "Of making many books there is no end," according to Ecclesiastes, and of making movies out of books there seems no end either. I get a bit edgy whenever I hear of yet another one being remodeled for film. Edgy not so much over what "they" will do to or with it, but rather over what I will do. "Are you going to see *A Little Princess*?" a friend inquires. Certainly not, is my visceral reply, but I pretend to think it over. And while pretending, I do in fact think. Why this intransigence, this unlovely refusal? For I can't bring myself to see the film version of *A Little Princess* any more than I could *Mr. and Mrs. Bridge* or *Housekeeping* or *The Heart Is a Lonely Hunter*, no matter how "faithful" or "sensitive" they are reputed to be. The terse chapters of Evan Connell's *Mr. Bridge* and *Mrs. Bridge*, an accumulation of searing episodes in limpid, uninflected sentences, seem especially uncongenial to movie treatment. Movies are pictures in motion, not designed to shape a patient and dazzling mosaic. And *Housekeeping* stays with me as an underwater dream, not something I would want to see dredged onto solid earth.

Least of all could I see *The Heart Is a Lonely Hunter*, which I read as an adolescent. Like *The Little Mermaid*, it turns on the ambiguities of speech, as well as the ramifying issues of human connection — nothing to do with the visual. Together with McCullers's troubled characters, I imagined the silence of Mr. Singer (canny name for a deaf-mute) as richly comprehending, a salvation from loneliness. I had fantasies of telling him my secrets too, and having them finally understood. What a shock to find that his all-embracing acceptance was pure silence — blank and neutral. That all along we had been talking to ourselves. It cast doubt even on those who give us back words: can we ever be understood? Or is language only an elaborate sustaining lie, every sentence a soliloquy? I knew even then I would have to pursue it anyway, but I could never again be quite sure my words weren't falling on deaf ears.

Despite all that, I don't much care for my purism about

filmed books. Or any purism, for that matter. What is it afraid of? What am I afraid of? The most ready answer is that I want to keep my own images, not have them replaced by a set designer's, nor have the characters take on the forms of actors I've seen before and will see again in other roles. A book's characters are not hollow molds to be filled by living flesh. They have more permanent forms — they are already embodied in words.

A commonplace objection, and cogent enough on the face of it, except it doesn't stand up to experience. In unsuccessful books-into-films, the images are usually too weak to do lasting harm. And in the successful ones I've been dragged to see — *Great Expectations, Howard's End,* Jean Rhys's *Quartet,* or Waugh's *A Handful of Dust* (obviously I'm not as pure as I'm claiming to be) — the actors for the most part "fit" the characters well. Even so, their images faded fast, leaving the books — my versions of the books — intact. The only film that has left its actors indelibly fixed in my mind is *Billy Budd,* and not a bad thing, as it turns out. My own imaging apparatus couldn't do better than Terence Stamp as the hapless Billy or Robert Ryan as Claggart (killed, I must constantly remind myself), not to mention Melvyn Douglas as the old Dansker and Peter Ustinov as Captain Vere; I feel quite comfortable with their faces shimmering through Melville's words. Meanwhile, *The Dead,* John Huston's triumph of literal and literary faithfulness, has all but vanished from my memory, leaving only an aura of truth, of Joyceness made visible. And perhaps that is as it should be. What must be conserved, after all, is not the integrity of the reader's vision but of the writer's. And since film is a flight of images through time, it is fitting that they should fly off, leaving the vision that is beyond ordinary imaging.

Which makes me wonder if I visualize at all as I read: Terence Stamp and Robert Ryan have not really replaced anything I can recall. Some readers may run their own private films as each page turns, but I seem to have only spotty fleeting images, a floaty gown, a sofa, a grand ballroom, or a patch of landscape. Language, that is, may lend itself to visual translation, but does not require it. It is its own universe of sound, rhythm, and connotation, which generate the occasional visual flare.

Not all books live by language or style, though: a host of other virtues — plot, situation, character, suspense, topical relevance — may keep them afloat. Galsworthy's *Forsyte Saga* or Armistead Maupin's *Tales of the City* fall into that genre and have made spectacular television series; I would have to be absurdly pure not to enjoy them. (*The Forsyte Saga* was so vivid that the actor Eric Porter could travel to remote parts of the world and find himself hailed on the street as Soames Forsyte. When he died recently I felt as if the unhappy Soames had died — a greater tribute, alas, than the actor might have wished.) In yet another genre, these days, are books written with the movie version in mind. But they are not properly books at all, just prefabricated scripts.

I've heard a thousand times that ours is a visual age. But I cannot uproot my passion for words for fashion's sake, even if I wanted to. I suppose what I fear is that movies, however ambitious and excellent, can never do for me what a book can do. (I seem, unwillingly or unwittingly, to have worked my way back to my — or my father's — ancient opposition of language and pictures. A picture is not worth a thousand words; it is worth only itself, as are the thousand words.) Films, to grant them their tony name, are an art form, but in my heart a movie is still a movie, an entertainment, a voyage in the dark, a plush seat, a bag of popcorn, Technicolor, air-conditioning, the most luscious of escapes. I do not ask that it feed my soul, only my fancy. When it does feed my soul — more often than I expect — I am surprised and grateful. Still, its words are not crucial or even many; new movies, with their visual elegance and slender scripts, use fewer words than ever. I know I should follow the story through the images, or rather follow the story *of* the images. But where, I keep wondering, is the story of the story?

It's clear even to me that my judgment is off the mark: movies are not competing with books but offering something else, a different sort of story. Why can't I appreciate each on its own terms? Because when I've read the book, I stubbornly don't want anything else. Why should I, when I've had the real thing, as originally conceived? Form and content are inseparable, and Greta Garbo, bewitching as she is, is not the Anna Karenina Tolstoy envisioned. If the form changes, the content must change.

Well, so what? Perhaps what I am afraid of is change itself. As if *Anna Karenina* could not withstand an ephemeral change! Can it be that I don't trust the works enough, that I secretly think them too flimsy to survive their adaptations? They are sturdier than I give them credit for. It must be my own responses that are not so sturdy: yes, there is always the danger that *they* might change on seeing an adaptation. So I catch myself out. Unwilling, it seems, to risk a new thought or feeling — like the people who won't read books in the first place, or yank them off the library shelves to protect the innocent.

Few, if any, stories are pure invention. Invention needs something to invent from, or with. Stories come from history, or from reality — lived or observed — or, as any quick survey will show, from other stories. But by my petulant logic I would refuse to see Racine's *Phèdre*, and Martha Graham's too. I would have to forswear much of Shakespeare, as well as *West Side Story* and Tennyson's *Ulysses* or Joyce's for that matter, not to mention Tchaikovsky's *Romeo and Juliet* and the host of paintings on classical themes, and on and on to absurdity.

Imagination is the refiner's fire; the sensibility of each new generation is the lens. Everything made has been transformed, just as language itself is translation from the inarticulate chaos within. To be a purist about adaptation is to attempt to halt an endlessly evolving process midway.

I didn't expect to argue a piece of my mind away. I should repent and repair to the movies. To A *Little Princess*. But will I have the courage?

Mʏ parents were people of the book but I did not appreciate this, and as I started college and acquired a dim sense of literary history, I indulged the adolescent's need to reshape them, to make them fit my ideal. I was sixteen. In the last gasp of identification with parents — which is often the first gasp of separation — I wanted them to share in the great discovery I was marveling at: that there *was* literary history, that the whole gorgeous landscape I had been flitting through at random, pausing here and there to sniff or taste or swallow, had an order, like a vast English garden. There were maps showing the paths and byways, replete with measurements and arrows, longitude and latitude, charts of the distances and relations between points. The college catalogue listed courses to choose from, to combine into patterns like the suggested tours in travel brochures. Sixteenth, Seventeenth, Eighteenth Century. Elizabethans, Augustans, Romantics, Victorians. (The moderns, unlike today, were given short shrift: anything current, it was implied, didn't require formal study — you could grasp it on your own.) Languages too: Anglo-Saxon, Old English, Middle English. Certain writers merited a course all to themselves: Chaucer, Shakespeare, Milton. As you progressed in an orderly fashion over four years, you would eventually cover every inch of the ground. I hadn't been so excited by the idea of scope and breadth since my first day of junior high school, when the Western History teacher announced that there had been something called the Renaissance in fifteenth-century Italy and listed its features on the blackboard. I had never heard of the Renaissance before. Even the word, Renaissance, was exalting, as was its companion word, "humanism." I was a humanist too, I decided that very day, and left school transformed.

The college catalogue was a similar awakening. Everything

I had been reading over the years was interconnected and fit into a larger design, as if it were all moving toward some grand culmination. I wanted to sample every century and take every course, like a greedy person at a buffet. I had never particularly needed my parents to share in my reading or in anything else I did. I was even rather secretive about my passions. But this discovery was too immense to keep to myself. No life could be complete, I thought, without studying the great works of Western literature. I began proselytizing at home. I burned with the zeal of a born-again reader; my bumper sticker would have proclaimed, Lit Saves.

I pressed books on my parents, cajoling or commanding, according to the mood of the hour. Though they didn't often read what I urged, they took the suggestions docilely, never challenging my campaign to educate them. In households where everyone criticizes everyone else, privileges accrue even to the youngest, if they can wait.

I had my greatest success with *The Trial*. It was not hard to get my father interested because it fit marginally into his preferred category of political books; also, he was a lawyer and the title promised legal proceedings. I was spending the Fourth of July weekend blissfully alone at home while my parents were in the country, the same dull country they had gone to every summer for as long as I could remember, my father part of the great caravan of men driving up for conjugal weekends. I had refused to go along when I was fifteen, and from then on I spent summers in the city, my father and I keeping house in our rudimentary way, mostly going out to dinner. The city in summer was a novelty, tropically languid, buildings misty with heat, air hushed and heavy, enervated streets. I had an office job. Each morning, I woke early, dressed in working-girl clothes, and rode the hot subway, and all these constraints I treasured as tokens of the independence I had craved since birth. My father didn't watch over my comings and goings; the most he asked was that I keep him company in air-conditioned movies every few nights, which was no hardship. Still, what I loved best were the weekends, when he disappeared and I could pretend I was living on my own. On one of those happy evenings, I received a long-distance call.

"That book you recommended," my father began with his customary abruptness. "By that Kafka. *The Trial.*" "Yes?" I said eagerly. "Did you read it?" "Well, that's what I'm calling you about. Your mother and I both read it and we have very different opinions on what it means. I say it's about the injustices of the legal system and the modern state, how you can get lost in the bureaucracy and red tape and so on. And she says it's just about life itself, how you're always guilty about something or other and you feel you deserve to be punished simply for being alive." He paused. My heart leaped. This was exactly what I wanted. We should theorize this way every waking hour.

"So?" he said, "what do you think?" My years of reading had brought forth fruit. I was an acknowledged expert on what things meant.

"Well, actually," I said in the cool, patronizing manner I had picked up from my professors, "you're both right. Those interpretations aren't mutually exclusive. The beauty of the book is that it can encompass so many points of view simultaneously."

My father was disappointed. He liked to have things one way or the other, and he liked to be right. He had probably been counting on me, for I usually supported his tough-minded as opposed to my mother's more humane, though no less sturdy, formulations. He argued his case for a while, then my mother got on the phone and pleaded hers, but I steadfastly refused to choose one over the other. They must have hung up vexed, but I was delighted, envisioning a future transformed. I would lead them through all of Western Lit, as I was being led, only a few steps ahead.

This never came to pass. In the fall I rented a room near school and began growing up. My life was no longer centered on home. What my parents read or didn't read stopped mattering. I had to learn to cook for myself. I asked my mother how come she had never taught me to cook; aside from using the meat grinder, all I knew were the grilled cheese sandwiches and cocoa and spaghetti in tomato and onion sauce from junior high. Why had she never trained me in the various housewifely arts for which I had had such scorn? She replied that I was always reading and she hadn't wanted to interrupt me.

I asked my parents if I might have a few of my favorite Harvard Classics in the black leather and gold trim, which had looked so intimidating when I graduated to my sister's room years earlier. Of course, they agreed. I might have convinced myself, in my intellectual pride, that I was finally ready for Plutarch's *Lives* or Virgil's *Aeneid*, but I knew in my heart that what I really wanted near me in my solitary room was volume 17, Grimm's and Andersen's fairy tales. And that was the one I couldn't find. I turned the house upside down, with no luck. It was lost, as if my passion had smothered it out of existence. I grieved, and it didn't help to know the stories could be found in libraries and bookstores: it was the particular volume that I grieved for. Then after a while I accepted the loss. The book became a memory, like a friend who died young, though at that stage of my life I had never had a friend who died young and didn't know what that felt like. This was the closest I came.

Long after, when I was fully adult, I mentioned my loss to a friend. She had inherited the same set from her parents, she said, and could easily give me her copy of volume 17. I was overjoyed, as if my dead friend had come back to life. So some losses are recoverable, I thought. The book she presented a few days later had the same gold trim, but instead of black leather it was a maroon or mahogany color. Not quite my old friend, even a bit of a violation. I hadn't known the Harvard Classics were issued in varied colors; that seemed a frivolity out of keeping with their sober mien. I had to amend my thinking: even if some losses are recoverable, what we recover may not be exactly the same. Still, I might as well be humble in accepting fate's gifts or I would have nothing but memories. I gave the new book a place on the shelf and willed myself to love it. When I passed by, I would gaze fondly at its mahogany spine and try to make it feel welcome, like a foster child — not my own flesh or adopted as my own flesh, but a stranger granted a temporary home — never letting it know that its warm maroon color reminded me of my loss, the stern black book. I didn't open it very often; it was enough to know I had it.

Just the other day I went to hunt it up and it was gone.

Maybe I loaned it to somebody (though I can't imagine doing that) or gave it to one of my children. But its loss seems curious and symbolic. Not that it felt itself insufficiently loved and therefore slipped away, no, nothing so mystical. Simply that I wasn't fated to keep it. The story of the book in the longer story of my life flouted the happy ending I had willed. It insisted on ending in real loss, which makes us treasure the intangible gifts of memory. For in the end, even if all my books were to vanish, I would still have them somewhere, if I had read them attentively enough. Maybe the words on the page are not even the true book, in the end, only a gateway to the book that recreates itself in the mind and lasts as long as we do.

In my solitary room near school I often ate alone and had the privilege of reading uninterrupted to my heart's content. I would feel myself once again — since only when you move on can you truly get anything back — sitting at the kitchen table reading *Heidi*, the book propped up on the flowered tablecloth and the old silver fork weighty in my hand. Whenever I eat alone and read, I retrieve the whole emotional apparatus that was mine before education and independence and all the experiences that make us unable to respond to books as children do.

Despite the lesson of the Harvard Classics volume 17, I can't help trying to recoup my losses. After my mother died, my sister and I went through her things and discovered the old meat grinder. We laughed at its primitiveness, recalling the endless grinding. "What shall we do with this old thing?" We had no use for it and tossed it out. Too hastily, for later on I would think of it with regret. And then there came a day when I saw one exactly like it at an outdoor flea market on Cape Cod. I seized it in a passionate embrace, almost staggering under the weight. I paid an absurd sum. When I got it home I didn't know what to do with it. I wasn't about to use it, yet it hadn't quite passed over into the realm of sculpture. I put it in a closet, where it remains. Sometimes in passing, I offer a nod of greeting. I like to think it might be the very same grinder I watched my mother use, and which she allowed me to use when she had the time and patience.

Through another gift of serendipity I also retrieved, just lately, a trace of *Miracle at Carville* — in the *New York Times*, of all places, the very medium of my childhood reading performances. A front-page article leaped toward my idle glance, reporting that the Gillis W. Long Hansen's Disease Center, known to the world as Carville, would probably close very soon. Only 130 patients remained, most of them elderly, and no new residents were being accepted. The article described life at Carville in its early years. What I had read as a boarding-school atmosphere had felt more like a prison, to which the sick were literally spirited away: if they refused to enter, they were forcibly taken by police or bounty hunters. Patients were incarcerated for life under rigid controls, including strict separation of the sexes. "The patients were not allowed to vote or to marry, and outgoing mail was steamed to sterilize it. Escapees were returned in handcuffs. Young women who got pregnant here were not allowed to keep their babies or even to touch them." Conditions eased slightly over time, as research undermined myths about Hansen's disease: for one thing, it is not very contagious. Today — as in Kalaupapa — despite their harsh memories, residents are not eager to leave what has become their only home.

One of those interviewed was Betty Martin, author of *Miracle at Carville*, who, like her heroine, married a fellow patient. They escaped through a hole in the fence but later returned for more treatment. Betty Martin's life, as sketched in the article, did not resemble the life I recalled from the book. Perhaps, in a writerly mode, she had made all that up. Or perhaps *I* made it up, my faulty memory falsifying her book: this would make me co-author of a book that never existed. Also the secret sharer of an imagined life, in a way even more convoluted than in my childhood.

I kept waiting, throughout the long article, for a mention of the book that had so ignited my imagination, but it never came. To this day, Betty Martin was labeled as a leper, but not as a writer. Even the name, Betty Martin, attached to her many monthly blood tests over the years, was not her original one. "We changed our names when we got here," she told the reporter, "to protect our families." The name was erased, the life thwarted. But the book remains.

On a long car trip some years ago, the kids in the back seat were restless — they were seven and four — and we had run through all our car-trip games. I found my mother's solution leaping to mind — the genes, in moments of weakness, reasserting themselves. But there was nothing in the car to sew and my daughters didn't know how to sew anyway; they would never make aprons and caps but would take woodworking and metal shop and bring home funny-shaped boxes of indeterminate use. "Why don't you teach her to read?" I burst out to the older one, hardly thinking of the implications, only that this would be a long project, longer than the car trip, surely. A few minutes later, having supplied pad and pencil, I heard her explaining the "at" family — cat and rat and fat and hat. (Why does it always start with the "ats"? Because cats and rats and hats figure prominently in nursery rhymes?) Some miles later it was the "an" family, and by the time we arrived, the "its" and "ots" and "ets" had been traversed. And so the younger one was launched on the perilous journey, crossing the bridge that can never be recrossed. I could only watch as mothers do when children leave home to seek their fortune, knowing that from now on her adventures would be beyond my ken, I could neither protect nor accompany her. The written word was about to carry her off like the tornado that took Dorothy.

I might have given her some good counsel about reading, except I had yet to find it out for myself. Just as every wine has its time, as a comically sober TV commercial used to inform us, so does every book. There are some we had better read while we are young, for their time will pass along with ours. Not that they're children's books; for a true reader, that sort of designation is immaterial, even arbitrary. *Little Women* has held up through several rereadings, and not through any cozy appeal to my putative inner child. It offers the same enduring qualities it always did: the allure of character shaping destiny, and a certain harmonious vision of personal evolution. Nor do books fail us — or we them — because they are fairy tales: as André Breton writes in *The Surrealist Manifesto*, calling for grown-up fairy tales, "The faculties do not change radically. Fear, the attraction of the unusual, chance, the taste for things extravagant are all devices which we can always call upon without fear of deception."

What we do leave behind are half-conscious paradigms of the world that we held tentatively, on spec, as it were. And if we love a book for its correspondence to one of these tentative visions, our love will evaporate along with our vision. I have not been able to take Hemingway seriously since my senior year of high school, when I wrote a heartfelt paper on *For Whom the Bell Tolls*. Since then, Hemingway imitations and parodies have become a fad among young writers, but to me Hemingway himself is the unmatchable parody. A sadder loss was *Tender Is the Night*, which won my eighteen-year-old heart; seductiveness is Fitzgerald's chief talent, and eighteen-year-olds are eminently seducible. Some twenty years later I decided it was time to revisit his work. *The Great Gatsby* was happily unaltered, or at least I was unaltered in relation to it. But some strange sea change had overtaken *Tender Is the Night*; I couldn't finish it; it had become a babble of silliness. It isn't, of course, only I have lost the exaggerated romanticism required to read it. I wish the book no ill. I hope exaggerated romanticism still thrives elsewhere.

Even though I shunned the movie of *The Heart Is a Lonely*

Hunter out of misbegotten loyalty, I can't say I reread Carson McCullers's books. I'm afraid I'd feel a certain dismay, like coming upon a photo of a great love of one's youth with the eyes of middle age. Imagine pining over that! Not that I'd find her books unworthy, just so oppressively *young*, so weighted by youth's Gothic glooms, manias, and succulent indulgences. Why violate all of that by my more stringent reading of to-day? No doubt it's my own Gothic glooms and adolescent manias — their purple afterglow — that I don't care to violate. I may be past them, but that is no reason to reject them.

(An opposite case is Willa Cather, who was standard high school reading in my day: teachers favored her direct language and presented the novels as healthful — like whole grains — and somehow patriotic. Yet Cather is the most adult of writers, full of irony and tragedy, of promise seeping away. Along with Robert Frost, she was for a long time mislabeled as benign, a tonic, and her work accordingly prescribed for the young.)

In a practical sense, too, books have their times; at the wrong moment, even great ones can prove as noxious as Mozart blaring from next door at two in the morning. While my father was in the hospital with cancer, I came home from a typical afternoon of watching him die slowly and idly plucked *The Death of Ivan Ilyich* from the shelf. What better distraction than Tolstoy? And high time I read such a famous work. (But was it such an idle choice? Maybe I didn't seek distraction at all but wanted to prolong the afternoon past visiting hours, for as long as I dwelt with my father's illness he was still alive.) The novella gives a graphically detailed account of a Russian bureaucrat's death from stomach cancer. That's what the reader sees, any-way; Ivan Ilyich is convinced until nearly the end, when it no longer matters, that he injured himself by falling from a lad-der while he hung the new dining-room curtains. Beyond the single case, it is about all of us — our misspent lives and pain-ridden deaths, exactly the sort of death I was witnessing; I hardly dared think about what sort of life. They say no girl was ever ruined by a book, but we can certainly be convulsed. *The Death of Ivan Ilyich* made me physically sick, yet I read on to the end, out of habit and fascination. A perverse yet fitting pleasure. The wrong book, but right too.

Others suffer from being untimely in a more provocative way. *A Little Princess*, spiritual guide of my childhood, is a highly conservative book in the best and worst senses. On its small scale, it exemplifies the extraliterary issues that are now heating up literary discussion. (Calling them extraliterary is, of course, fanning the flames.) To bristle at *A Little Princess's* superannuated politics — the strict class stratification, the co-lonial attitudes toward India — would be to deny its organizing principle: disrupting the status quo by casting the heroine into poverty and pain, only to set it right again. This is precisely what yields its special radiance and harmony. What *is* hard to take is the complacent acceptance of social inequity. Mr. Carrisford, a charitable Victorian, muses, "How many of the attics in this square are like that one, and how many wretched little servant girls sleep on such beds, while I toss on my down pillows, loaded and harassed by wealth that is, most of it — not mine." But his friend Mr. Carmichael, the lawyer, "cheerily" offers balm for the conscience: "If you possessed all the wealth of all the Indies, you could not set right all the discomforts of the world." And that is that. It's not their politics that puts me in an extraliterary quandary. It's their nonchalance.

In Irving Howe's last book of essays, *A Critic's Notebook*, a few scattered references to Henry James's *The Awkward Age* made the novel sound so intriguing that I promptly got hold of a copy. How could I have missed it, I wondered, in my period of James worship? I thought I'd covered that territory pretty thoroughly. Starting in college and continuing for maybe ten years, I had watched the world through James's eyes, so powerfully contagious was his vision. I saw my web of family and friends as a Jamesian "situation" — one of his favorite words; I analyzed the various life stories proceeding around me as he might analyze them; I even tried matchmaking in his characters' cunning spirit. In my plottings, no vast fortunes or weighty moral issues were at stake, but I could pretend they were. Life was full of subtleties, the very air around each utterance pulsing with implication; simple encounters would provide material for endless speculation, and while I refrained from speaking a Jamesian language in the office where I worked as a typist or with old friends who might think I had been visited by aliens, I spun my private thoughts in orotund Jamesian sentences laden with digressive subordinate clauses, so as to ensnare every conceivable aspect of a subject, regardless of how minute.

It couldn't last, naturally. Who had the time? There was actual life to be lived, with its press of jobs, children, school, grocery shopping, and repairmen, most of which never appear in a James novel. James's world, as he no doubt knew better than any reader, is a world of the mind, of embattled intellectual and emotional constructs, not a reflection of physical realities. My coming to this truth did not at all diminish him as writer; if anything, it made his artifices more subtle. But it did leave me free to read and write and live by my own lights. So now I could approach *The Awkward Age* not as an acolyte, just a reader looking for a good time.

I began with the Preface. It was impenetrable. This was very odd, since I had read most of James's Prefaces years back for my master's thesis on his novels. Possibly I had lost brain cells. And yet over the intervening years I had managed to read many books as well as write a number of my own — it was unlikely that my language faculties were impaired. Never mind. I flipped to the first page. This, thank goodness, was not impenetrable. No, it fairly breezed along, as James might say. It was interesting, it was lively, it was even clear as far as subject goes, not that I was ever a stickler for immediate clarity. Except I couldn't believe any people anywhere, at any time, could ever speak such sentences.

Had they spoken that way in the other novels? Yes and no. They — the Jamesites, we may call them, since they hail from a far country all their own — had always had an unearthly command of extemporaneous speech, but now they sounded even more airy and elliptical, or at least it seemed so to one who hadn't traveled among them for a while. *I* knew what they were talking about because I was the reader, immersed in a book whose plan and purpose I had some inkling of, but how did *they* know what they were talking about? Had I been in their drawing rooms, I wouldn't have had a clue.

It's true that James was attempting something unusual in *The Awkward Age*: he denies himself nearly all the rites of narration, description, and commentary (not that those ever helped characters understand each other) and instead relies heavily on dialogue. As a result, the novel often reads like a play, a form he tried all his life to master but whose economies were very unsuited to his gifts. He also concocts a deliberate obscurity, as Irving Howe points out: everyone in those drawing rooms is meant to be somewhat in the dark about their friends' motives and desires. Very much like life, in other words.

And very exasperating. But I wasn't bored; I read on, and little by little I gave in, allowing myself to be entranced all over again. He was a genius, I had to admit. But not the same kind of genius he had been when I was a graduate student. The characters in *The Awkward Age* simply didn't care enough about ordinary human fulfillments — love, sex, work — to be credible. Even money, which elsewhere in James is taken very seriously, is secondary. What they do care about exclusively — the "good" characters at any rate — is the moral design of their lives. Even to a James fan, this is hardly like life. When I was young, with the luxury to think life was propelled by moral designs, I thought he knew everything. I defended him against the charge that his characters had no appetites. On the contrary, I said, their appetites were the hidden root of all the action. But I was mistaken. Now I had to acknowledge ruefully that there were things even the master did not know. This discovery is not liberating but limiting: if even genius has its blind spots, what hope is there for the rest of us?

CHILDREN generally read what they please, but addictive adults (writers especially) can get tangled in the toils of choice. There may be as many kinds of reading as there are books, each one demanding its own form and degree of active participation; our choices can depend on whether we relish the exertions of volleyball, as it were, or prefer a meandering round of croquet. A writer like Henry Green, for example, sets down the merest hints on the page, leaving us practically to write the book ourselves, the way archaeologists reconstruct a tomb from three chunks of stone and a dip in the ground. Others, George Eliot, say, make us feel a trifle superfluous. We come ready to do our share, only to find that the author, like a solicitous mother, has anticipated our every need and errant fancy. I'll choose the coddling every time, yet more spartan types rave of the beauties of Henry Green, about whom I feel as I do about marathon running: I'd like to do it, but I just haven't the constitution.

At times the ramifications of choice verge on the metaphysical, the moral, even the absurd. To read the dead or the living, the famous or the ignored, the kindred spirits or the brac-

ingly unfamiliar? And how to go about it — systematically or
at random?

At bottom, of course, the issue in choosing what to read (and
what to do and how to live) is the old conflict, dating from the
Garden, of pleasure versus duty: what we want to read versus
what we think we ought to read, or think we ought to want
to read. Set out this way, it seems a simple distinction. And
the extremes are indeed simple — books I am paid to review,
as opposed to unheralded, unfashionable books I gravitate to
like a respectable businessman shuffling into a porn movie
house. In between lie acres of ambiguity, the many books (the
many acts) I cannot in all decency leave unread (undone) —
or can I?

An unusually clear case some years ago was Katherine Anne
Porter's *Ship of Fools*. Reviews proliferated like cells splitting
in an embryo; literary pages were monopolized for weeks.
(Pity any less celebrated author whose book appeared at the
same time.) Yet something put me off. Beyond the reported
twenty-year gestation period and the arrogance of its metaphor
(such relentless meaning), it was the awe that greeted it, an awe
more fit for hugenesses like the Grand Canyon, and which
made it obligatory reading. How to escape? In conversation, I
lay low. Lying, as I mentioned earlier, was out of the question.
But you can always say you haven't read something "yet." "Yet"
extended longer and longer, like string from a spool. I still
haven't read it, but the "yet" is gone — I let go the string. I
waited it out.

Much of the time, though, the distinction is not simple at

all — at least I am not among the happy few who can readily distinguish want from ought. We are taught from our first breath to want what others think we should want. They dress up "ought" in the insidious garb of want, a wolf in sheep's clothing, so that life's greatest task becomes the unmasking of false desire to reveal the bleak bare-toothed ought, and the unearthing of true desire.

Aside from the magazine pieces, the authors I read as a child were dead, and I still fancy the dead, a taste nowadays almost dowdy. To read current books, in our age detached from history, is to be forever young, forward-looking, partaking of the merciless energy of daybreak joggers and successful deal makers, rubbing shoulders with celebrity writers. (Could Villon or Baudelaire have dreamed writers would join the ranks of the beautiful people?) Current books are modishly sleek inside and out, low-fat, low-cholesterol, sort of like Lite beer — not bad on a hot day yet hardly the thing for a seasoned drinker. Meanwhile the books of the dead stay heavy and dun-colored, their pages not quite white, their typefaces stolid and ingenuous (except for those fortunate few treated to brand-new paperback attire, like a face-lift or hair implant). Reading the dead is being a meat-eater in a vegetable age, mired in superseded values. When someone at a dinner party asks, Read any good books lately?, *Jane Eyre* or *Pamela* is not a fertile answer. These are closed issues, closed books. (Although nowadays the question is more apt to be, Seen any good films lately? This shift illustrates the much-noted decline of the printed word and the ascendancy of screens bearing images. The common currency of getting-acquainted discourse, or even of discourse between friends, is no longer about what we are reading and thinking, but what we are seeing. A pity that they should have to be rivals.)

The pressure to read the living is moral as well as social. We must know our own times, understand what is happening around us. But I know my own times. I am in them. I have only to walk down Broadway or Main Street to see what is happening. It is the times of the dead I do not know. The dead are exciting precisely because they are not us. They are what we will never know except through their books. Their trivia are our exotica. As writers, transmitters, the dead can be more alive than some of the living.

I can hear the protests: I am romanticizing, not even granting the dead their proper context but allowing distance to contour and laminate them. Today's living will someday acquire that fine airbrushed otherness. Why not be daring and appreciate them now? Besides, the dead writers have been preselected; no discrimination is necessary. I needn't sift through five dozen nineteenth-century Russian novelists and decide, okay, this arrogant, tormented count, this loony gambler with the dubious past, this dapper smooth fellow, that sweet country doctor. I am forfeiting the opportunity to judge, to rank, to shape the tradition.

The question of judgment, of who is worth reading and what constitutes the tradition, has grown difficult and complex. Until lately it was assumed automatically that the writers whose works endured were the most significant. With the spur of feminist criticism, with the freeing of vision to include literatures other than Western and attitudes other than white and male, the idea of the "canon" has come under cross-examination — not only its contents but the notion of an exclusive body of "the enduring" or "the best." Who has chosen the revered works and by what standards? What has escaped their vision? How do such decisions and rankings encourage some voices and discourage others? Above all, how does a biased literary tradition cramp our present and future reading and writing?

These are not new issues by any means, but they need to be reexamined with each shift in social circumstances. For very possibly the canon of great works does not emerge naturally from history, but our view of history from a fairly arbitrary canon, in which case the way to a truer history is through a more inclusive tradition. The familiar dead have brought us to where we are. But supposing we wish to take ourselves to a different place? What if our forms of political action and discourse had been determined not by reading Machiavelli, but, say, Confucius or Lao-tzu?

Being truly current (not merely low-fat) demands that we resurrect or re-emphasize works — by the dead and the living — overlooked through faulty vision, which is presently being done by scholars and editors. It does not mean, though, that the canonized dead must be crowded out because others join them. In art there is no problem of space. The road is broad and forever under construction, as Eliot has pointed out, forever being refurbished and widened. With the advent of each new writer who will someday be "dead" in my romantic sense — a García Márquez or Gordimer or Coetzee or Calvino — it undergoes major alteration. Every writer's work is changed. Not that we are influenced in any specific or even noticeable way, but that we work with an awareness of new lanes, new curves, and new road signs.

On a small island off the coast of Spain I met an American writer, an expatriate, if the term still applies — he had not been stateside in many years. He had never heard of Raymond Carver. A good or a bad thing? I wondered. It definitely mattered one way or the other, as it might not have mattered centuries ago. Whatever Carver's work means decades from now, today it signifies a development, a provocative shift. If the man I met was a genius, I decided, a Shakespeare or Sophocles, the gaps in his knowledge would matter very little: he would go his own way, creating his context out of genius, not temporal conditions. (Though what would Shakespeare have been like without his Italian forebears?) But if he was simply a good and serious writer, he ought to know.

The more purposeful a writer is, the more her work defines a particular connection to her time and surroundings. Or, if "defines" sounds a bit deadly, let's say "shows," for no writer consciously sets out to do it (or does so at her peril). The connection is evident in the writing to the degree that it is strong in the writer. If she does not feel context — time, place, spirit — pressing in on her like humidity, the work will be ephemeral and self-referential, brittle as a fallen leaf. Part of context is what other writers are doing with the same context.

So despite my necrophilia, I read the living to know in what terms the connections are being illustrated. Then I can use, abuse, or neglect these terms in full consciousness. For inevitably, every living writer is a part of every other, all of us bumping up against each other like passengers in a loaded bus. Some feel and smell better than others, and we may wish certain ones would just disembark, but for the moment they must be taken account of. When there is a pothole in the road, we are all jolted.

I can vacillate lengthily, and foolishly, over whether to read at random (as I did on my bed in the fading light) or in some programmed way (as we all did in school). I like to cling to the John Cage-ish principle that if randomness determines the universe it might as well determine my reading too; to impose order is to strain against the nature of things. Randomness continuing for long enough will yield its own pattern or allow a pattern to emerge organically, inscrutably, from within — or so I hope. On the other hand, how comforting to have a plan. It harks back to the satisfaction of pleasing authority and earning a gold star. With a few months' effort, anyone can become an expert on Balzac or medieval epics or Roman comedies, and how reassuringly American, too, are expertise, thoroughness, inclusiveness — offshoots of manifest destiny, no doubt, the need to control the entire territory.

The case of random versus order is an old duality among the many that Western thought likes to ease into, safe harbors after the tossings of ambiguity, just as nineteenth-century symphonies, after fretful harmonic uncertainty, resolve into their tonic chords, somewhat begging the question, it seems. Isaiah Berlin, in *The Hedgehog and the Fox*, quotes the Greek poet Archilocus: "The fox knows many things, but the hedgehog knows one big thing," meaning that hedgehogs connect everything to one all-embracing principle, while foxes "entertain ideas that are centrifugal rather than centripetal . . . seizing upon a vast variety of experiences and objects for what they are in themselves." The quote may be read more literally and mundanely too. The hedgehog knows one thing — physics or ballet or the movements of the tides — and therefore knows the world, for nature works the same patterns everywhere, with surface variations; while the fox is a quite respectable dilettante, knowing the huge range of variations, with a smattering of methodology.

Swift divided writers into spiders and bees, the one buzzing from flower to flower gathering their diverse sweetnesses to transform into uniform honey, the other gazing inward, spinning elaborate, sticky webs out of the dirty stuff of the self. And yet true contemplatives are not self-absorbed in Swift's scorned and narrow sense. The Zen master, sitting and breathing, sees, or will see eventually, the whole world via the emptiness (readiness) of the self, the world compellingly real and multiform, flashing into the receptive eye.

I tend to think writers — and readers too — may be spiders *and* bees, foxes *and* hedgehogs, depending on mood and timing and need. I spent a hedgehog winter years ago reading the Greek tragedies. There are many good reasons to read them.

Mine was that I had ordered a set from a discount catalogue. Anything acquired in such a carefree way — sitting at the desk, a mere matter of pen and paper — must be used, to justify the indulgence. All the frosty season I lived with royalty, amid high tragedy. Clearly, life was not the endless trivia it sometimes appeared to be, but a struggle of principle and impulse, passion and duty bearing down on primal family bonds. Yet for all we know, while gouging out Oedipus's eyes, even Sophocles had his own on the clock for the moment when he had to go to the fishmonger or write a recommendation for a promising student or drive his mother-in-law to the dentist. Without biography, which cannot help but take its subjects down a peg or two, we are free to imagine him dwelling nobly in the realms of tragedy. So reading ennobles life, or at least makes noble illusions possible.

Without any calculated plan, though, I read every novel by Jean Rhys and Barbara Pym as soon as I could get my hands on them. It was like eating candy — the chocolate-covered nuts of the cinema or the celebrated potato chips of which you can't eat just one. The variations in their novels were in fact no more than the slightly different planes and convolutions in each potato chip, and each one predictably tasty. I became an expert in self-indulgence.

When, every so often, I have a spasm of needing to get organized, I make lists of books to read. In between reading the books on the list I am sidetracked by the books pressed on me by friends, or the shelved books suddenly demanding loudly, after much postponement, to be read right away, or the piles of books arriving in the mail with notes from editors beseeching that I read them. If they only knew the convoluted agonies of choice!

Except for a few that capture my fancy, these last can be skimmed or shelved or passed on to the needy. But the urgings of dear friends — "You must read this, I loved it" — present a graver problem. They refer to more than books; they are an index of the friendship's value and durability. Although sharing a love of the same books is affirmation of a friendship, not sharing it may be an even stronger testimony. "You wouldn't like it, it's not your kind of thing," is a happy sign that the friend understands, as well as a reprieve. But when she raves about a book, what else to say but, yes, thank you. For us conscientious types, the words become a pledge of the same order as, "I'll be there to hold your hand before the surgery," or "Sure I'll take the kids so you can meet him" — IOUs we must be ready to have called in. Luckily, our friend often forgets the book or gets excited about a new one. We may escape with reading one in four, we may well love them. What I love for certain, though, is listening to the friend talk about the book, sometimes the best part.

Months, even years, go by. I return to my list to find I've read perhaps a third of the books on it, not bad, under the circumstances. But by then I am a new person, with a new list under way. The unread books get carried over, and over, until eventually I cross them out. They are no longer necessary. I can hardly recall what allure they held for the person I used to be. Still, drawing a line through a title feels like inflicting a flesh wound — that much of me remains the same.

I am glad, at heart, of the inefficiency of my reading lists. Who wants to be an efficient reader? For a short time I was one, or was expected to be. Besides cooking and The Apartment, in the junior high smorgasbord we called "departmental" was another new course: Library. Twice a week we repaired to an unusually pleasant room for a public school at that time — big windows, lots of light, thriving plants, walls lined with books, blond wood tables comfortably seating six. Maybe memory embroiders — it sounds too lovely.

SPEECH IS SILVER BUT SILENCE IS GOLDEN, said the sign on the library wall. What bizarre alloy did this make of reading, a form of silent speech? On the first day, the librarian, a gentle gray-haired woman with no special subject to impart and thus no anxious fervor, told us to choose a book from the shelves, any book, and sit and read it. This was familiar, I did it all the time at home. But I had never done it in a room with thirty other people. In fact, reading was about the last activity I would have associated with school. For those forty-five minutes, school took on a homey feel. I got absorbed, as I did curled on my bed, and almost forgot the surroundings. But not entirely. Any private pleasure appropriated by an institution is in danger of losing its savor, and alas, reading took on an official tinge.

The librarian taught us how to keep a chart of our reading. A narrow column for the date, a wide one for the title of the book, one for the author, and finally, one to note the pages read. It had not occurred to me that the number of pages, the rate, mattered. What could quantity have to do with reading? Yet from that moment there it was, sour and inescapable. In college we groaned ritually over long reading lists — how to get it all done? We calculated our speeds in different subjects (fifty pages an hour for a novel, thirty for history, twenty for philosophy) and parceled out our time. It is a blasphemous way to read, like a Black Mass, mocking the act by denaturing it. What a mercy it was to finish with school and be able to read again.

When I can't remember what I read last week or mean to read tomorrow, I think of keeping better lists, and keeping to them. Then I recall that sour old library chart recording prowess. Better to forget than to chart. Anything I really need will spring to mind sooner or later: chance is provident.

That is to say, reading at random — letting desire lead — feels like the most faithful kind. In a bookstore, I leaf through the book next to the one I came to buy, and a sentence sets me quivering. I buy that one instead, or as well. A book comes in the mail and I begin it out of mild curiosity, to finish spellbound. A remark overheard on a bus reminds me of a book I meant to read last month. I hunt it up in the library and glance in passing at the old paperbacks on sale for twenty-five cents. There is the book so talked about in college — it was to have prepared me for life and here I have blundered through decades without it. Snatch it up quickly before it's too late. And so what we read is as wayward and serendipitous as any taste or desire. Or perhaps randomness is not so random after all. Perhaps at every stage what we read is what we are, or what we are becoming, or desire.

To recognize desire is itself a reading of the body. Every twinge and throb, every quickening of the pulse and melting of the muscles is a message to be deciphered. As infants we read such messages instinctively, then quickly forget how. Learning to read words on the blackboard echoes that early, crucial reading of ourselves. It feels familiar, *déjà vu*. But because it starts with figuring out signs and giving proper answers, we mistake its nature for cerebral. On the contrary, true reading is sensuous: words, with their freight of connotation, speed through us unrestrained, suggesting unimagined possibilities, a future cut loose from settled expectations. And once the mind is set free by that dashing, dazzling act of reading, the recognizing of desire — unmasking the false and unearthing the true — can become instantaneous again, like not having to move your lips or sound out the words. The whole body, radiating from the heart, is attuned to sensation, waves us on or warns us off like a semaphore. We cannot always follow, but at least we are not deluded, at least there is clarity. We know how to read anew, to distinguish our own signs and meanings.

Quite the opposite is reading to confirm what we already know, who we have resolved or consented to be. Yes, we nod, settling the brain into a stiff smugness, that's pretty much what I thought I'd find. Naturally. We would find it anywhere, because we bring it with us. Readers with a particular agenda to support or advance — Marxists, Freudians, feminists, to name the strongest — are most susceptible, for reading this way clarifies and reinforces ideology. But everyone does it to some extent. My parents did it when reading *The Trial*, as I did when I urged it on them, for with my agenda at the time, value was conferred by being listed in a college catalogue. In this seductive mode we are not so much reading as rewriting. The book is not happening to us; we are happening to it. It is to a book's greatest credit that it can withstand such repeated onslaughts and remain serenely intact, ready for the next assailant or, with luck, the next reader.

That brand of reading has nurtured the popular critical distinction between text and subtext. When I hear books called texts I feel a pang, as if family treasures were being relegated to the distant airless safe-deposit box. Who ever curled up happily to spend the evening with a text? For that matter, what writer ever set out to write one? The critics would reply that the work becomes a text once it leaves the writer's hands, but isn't that a form of sophistry? Even the Supreme Court has acknowledged that the fate of a work of art and the uses to which it may be put belong in the control of the artist.

No, the businesslike use of the word "texts" for stories or poems is undeniably punitive, dismissive. We address people more formally than usual when we feel disapproval or distaste; we take an aloof tone with irksome children. Just so coolly does Prince Hal cut Falstaff, and the audience winces.

What is wrong with being unashamedly a novel or a poem? What offense could they have committed to so alienate the critics? Clearly the poor work of imagination has sunk to demimondaine status, someone we might relish visiting in private, like Swann with Odette, but cannot publicly acknowledge — although Swann, man of the heart as he is, not only acknowledged Odette eventually but married her, which in critical circles would be the equivalent of Jacques Derrida's confessing he simply adored a certain novel, he couldn't quite justify it but it touched his heart. This would be a little foolish and impractical, it could cause talk and snickers, yet it would open the door of a stifling room to some fresh air.

I first heard the companion word, "subtext," used around writing workshops. I was puzzled, but briefly; it is not an opaque word, not one you need to look up in the O.E.D. If there is a text, naturally there can be a subtext. A peculiar tendency of Western thought is that everything sooner or later is perceived in terms of surface and subsurface; we rarely trust that what we see is the real or the entire thing. Like paranoiacs, behind an innocuous surface we infer a threatening intent (seldom the other way around). We love tales of disrobing (Salomé), of unmasking, of mistaken identity. Of course many things are obscure and require penetration. I am not suggesting we stop at immediate impressions, merely that positing a hierarchy of surface and subsurface can complicate perception. What is hidden does not arise from a built-in perversity or coyness in the nature of things (or books). The veil may be in our eyes. In Eastern thought both the apparent and the obscure are immanent. Nothing is "wrong" or tricky with the way things present themselves. If we look keenly enough for long enough, it is all there.

The paradigm of text and subtext suggests that while a book seems to be about such and such — how Pip encounters the great world and learns the vanity of ambition, how Emma Bovary is ruined by illusion, how Macbeth descends, act by act, from human to brute — beneath the story line is something else, probably undercutting the surface. All fully realized works are about exactly what they are about.

"Text" and "subtext" are more fitting for analyzing dreams than writing. We accept that the dream images and events are not "really" what the dream is about, but the available detritus of the day, slyly adapted to shield the dream's actual "meaning." Writing is not dreaming. True, we must write about *something*. There must be events and images and furniture to occupy reader and writer while the elusive other thing — the idea, the book's *raison d'être* — snakes its way along. But the beauty of a story, unlike a dream, is that the screen of events and furniture becomes primary. The original, embryonic idea, if there is one, adapts to fit their shape, rather than the reverse. So a novel is finally about the things of this world, a world of things.

The poet Adam Zagajewski would go even farther, to claim that there is no elusive other thing, no embryonic idea, nothing but the cold transparency of poetry, nothing but the inner life seeking to express itself. "It uses cunning," he writes in "The Untold Cynicism of Poetry."

> It pretends that it is interested, oh yes, very interested in external reality. . . . War? Terrific. Suffering? Excellent. . . . Reality is simply indispensable; if it did not exist, one would have to invent it. Poetry attempts to cheat reality; it pretends that it takes reality's worries seriously. It shakes its head knowingly.

In the end, he finds reality "only a bottomless source of metaphors for poetry." Zagajewski's view is provocative. There is not a writer alive or dead who has not felt the profound care-

lessness he describes, and the exhilaration it brings. But along
with the inner life, there is — there must be — the story itself,
with its own inner life that occupies the vast spaces of our own.
In a novel, that story infuses and penetrates the screen of reality until there is only the rich surface. Or if that sounds too frivolous, there is only wholeness, immanence.

For purposeful, dutiful reading, the reading of
"texts," we apply a special sort of concentration, special because it is applied. Willed. Such reading may be pleasant, but
it is pleasant work, the kind of work I can easily and dutifully
do in the daylight hours. It goes fast because we are looking for
something rather than allowing something to happen. When
waiting for something to happen we never move fast, hardly
move at all. Between the turning of the pages, eons pass. We
drift suspended in the words, all stillness and expectancy. Concentration is effortless yielding, as I yielded while sitting on my
bed under the casement windows that opened on the rows of
tiny backyards, not noticing the fading of the light until the
words got fuzzy on the page.

I am still a slow reader, but when I read to be informed, the
pages fly by. There is no need to adapt to the style (there often
is no style to speak of), no need to wrap myself in it, to tune
my ear to the timbre of another voice. For here is the essence
of true reading: learning to live in another's voice, to speak another's language. Reading is escape — why not admit it? — but

not from job or troubles. It is escape from the boundaries of our own voices and idioms.

My reading is more restless and volatile than ever these days. I pick up something on a subject I care about, only to find myself yawning five minutes later. Or else at four in the morning I seek something dull to relieve insomnia — the fluctuations of the economy or the latest statistics on population growth — and contrary to all expectation I'm totally absorbed. What keeps me so wide awake is the ardor and animation of the writer's mind at work, or better still, at play. Few subjects are inherently dull: language is where dullness or liveliness resides. Subject, it seems, is little more than a bridge to something more crucial. Which recalls Adam Zagajewski: if the writer, careless of subject, is simply seeking a means to express the inner life, the reader may be engaged in a parallel quest — not for an appealing subject but for the affinity of a congenial mind. Yet mind alone is not enough; it must move skillfully in a field of words.

The good writer offers a new language, the silent language of the inner voice, the silver and the gold. He tries on lingos and accents as we all do in private, and invites us to the startling intimacy of hearing him talk to himself with abandon, camping it up, doing all the voices. For all its originality, *Finnegan's Wake* makes flagrantly explicit what has always been a tacit strategy of fiction. It is not the use of a private language *per se* that distinguishes Joyce, but its rare lexicon and his refusal to translate.

Imagine Whitman's contemporaries first coming upon his

poems. Surely the biggest shock would have been how he han-
dled the first person pronoun, giving it the place of honor as
well as a magnetism that draws every other word into its orbit.
It is a syntactical shock, jolting the sense of order and placement. In Proust the shape of a sentence — tenses and clauses
intricately braided — prefigures the entire structure of past
and present interpenetrating, supporting each other. From
Faulkner to Gertrude Stein to Virginia Woolf, the writers who
claim our attention do so by voice and idiom, which are the
audible manifestations of the mind. This is how it sounds inside, they declare. Listen, hear the shape with me. There is
good reason for the addictive cravings of readers: the only new
thing under the sun is the sound of another voice. Hearing
it truly, we know what Shunryu Suzuki, in *Zen Mind, Beginner's Mind*, calls "not just ordinary language, but language in
its wider sense." This language is hardly interference but — to
return to the much put-upon Mr. Cha — a way of keeping the
mind free.

By the same token, it is the abdication of voice that makes
some authors irredeemably dull, regardless of clever plots or
exotic settings. Dull writers use a generalized, undistinguished
language, not an inner language in the making. Some have
lost faith in language altogether and use as little as they can get
away with. (Why are they writing? To illustrate the failure of
language?) Ben Jonson said, "Speak, that I may know thee."
But dull writers refuse to speak. Someone or something is
speaking through them, maybe a newspaper or television
voice, or maybe our very own voices, as the writers infer us to

be. They hope to give us to ourselves, to mirror their times —
but mimicking is not mirroring.

Speak, that I may know thee, we implore those who address
us publicly, from television news anchors to political candi-
dates. But none will oblige. Do they find it unseemly or scary
or inconvenient, or what? Do they use prefab phrases to their
children, their friends, their lovers? Have any of them, lately,
spoken a sentence bearing the shape of the thought that inspired it? Or do they no longer think? This is Orwell territory,
and in fact the prophesy of "Politics and the English Language" has come true in our political discourse. It became gro-
tesquely apparent during the Watergate episode, and since
then the words emanating from Washington fulfill it every day.
Hardly any elected officials can or will reveal a genuine voice,
and those who try hardest to be all things to all people are the
most pathetic. In their staggering feats of self-erasure, they are
a warning to writers who try to mirror their times. Such writers
may end by becoming invisible; the mirror they hold up will
be blank.

When I began, I thought reading would transform my life, or
at least teach me how to live it. It does teach something, many
things, but not what I naively expected. In the thick of experience, snatches of bookish wisdom do not serve. If no girl was
ever ruined by a book, none was ever saved by one either.
(Even less useful is looking to fictional characters. The best of
them travel in confusion and come to a bad end: this is what
makes their lives worth inventing. It is we, the readers, who

have the counseling role. Do this, do that, we tell them. Don't forget to mail that letter, don't get on that plane. Divorce him, marry her, look over your shoulder for heaven's sake. But to no avail.)

So what has been the point? Not to amass knowledge, since I forget the contents of books. Certainly not to pass the time, or "kill" it, as some say. (Time will kill us.) For killing is jumping the gun, so to speak. We "kill" time to leap over its body to a future event, if only dinner. But after dinner we find, like Macbeth, that we must kill some more, till the next event. Plainly the events are just a more dramatic means of killing. What we are waiting for, killing time to arrive at, is death, the only event that can release us from the burden of living time. Killing time is to living what Evelyn Wood's speed-reading is to reading, sprinting as opposed to leisurely walking, where you can appreciate the scenery. The goal is to get it over with, to no longer have to do it. (Speed-reading is not actually reading at all but eye exercises.)

The underside of killing time is rushing about, going and doing in order to feel that each moment is actively, assertively "lived" — merely another bout with mortality. Reading is an activity of the moment too; having read is no more palpable than yesterday's feast. But unlike classic activities of the moment, dance or sports or sex — movement through phases — in reading, the body is still. Indeed what reading teaches, first and foremost, is how to sit still for long periods and confront time head-on. The dynamism is all inside, an exalted, spiritual exercise so utterly engaging that we forget time and mortality along with all of life's lesser woes, and simply bask in the ever-lasting present. So I see, finally, why it hardly matters whether I remember the contents of the book. Mere information is nothing compared to this silent flurry. The mind comes into its own, delighting in its litheness and power; it pirouettes, leaps for the ball, embraces and trembles. Outwardly we are languid. We have made the preparations Calvino advises in the opening pages of *If on a Winter's Night a Traveler*:

> Find the most comfortable position: seated, stretched out, curled up, or lying flat. . . . Stretch your legs, go ahead and put your feet on a cushion, on two cushions, on the arms of the sofa, on the wings of the chair, on the coffee table, on the desk, on the piano, on the globe. Take your shoes off first. . . . Adjust the light so you won't strain your eyes. Do it now, because once you're absorbed in reading there will be no budging you. . . . Try to foresee now everything that might make you interrupt your reading. Cigarettes within reach, if you smoke, and the ashtray. Anything else? Do you have to pee? All right, you know best.

We gaze at marks on a page, put there by a machine, recognizable as words. Each one denotes something discrete but we do not, cannot, read them as such, except in the first days of learning how. They offer themselves in groups with wholes greater than the sum of the parts. As in human groups, the individual members behave in relation to their companions: each word presents aspects of itself suited to the ambiance, amplifying some connotations and muting others. Their respective rankings must change too. A word will be key here, play a supporting role there, and in each successive appearance will be weightier and more richly nuanced. All this we register faster than the speed of the light illuminating our page, hardly aware of noting the valence, assessing the role and position, of each word as it flies by, granting it its place in the assemblage.

Still more remarkable, these inky marks generate emotion, even give the illusion of containing emotion, while it is we who contribute the emotion. Yet it was there in advance too, in the writer. What a feat of transmission: the emotive powers of the book, with no local habitation, pass safely from writer to reader, unmangled by printing and binding and shipping, renewed and available whenever we open it.

Semioticists have unraveled these miracles in detail; even to call them miracles sounds ingenuous. After all, most aesthetic experience rests on transference through an inanimate medium. What is painting but oils smeared on canvas, or chamber music but bows drawn across strings? Reading is not the same, though. There is no sense organ that words fit like a glove, as pictures fit the eye or music the ear. Intricate neural transactions take place before words find their elusive target, before the wraith we call the "writer" finds the reader.

For dwelling in the book, however remote in time and space, is this imaginary being, this missing link whom no reader has ever glimpsed. Yes, from the visits of Dickens and Wilde to today's performances, readers flock to see writers, to meet the person who has given them pleasure; perhaps the consumers of telephone sex also yearn to meet the purveyors. But they are sure to be disappointed. The writer "in person" is no more the voice behind the book than the employee who murmurs salacious tidbits is inclined to stir us in actual life. Like the owner of the telephone voice, the writer is born of our fantasies. Reading her book, we fashion her image, which has a sort of existence, but never in the flesh of the person bearing her name.

Since the book, too, doesn't possess an independent or sensory existence but must be opened and fathomed, we enjoy the heady power of being necessary to its life. The real book is the prince hidden inside the frog. We open it, and our eyes give the kiss of regeneration. This power is what intoxicates. The thinking of others does not interfere with our own free thinking, but meshes with it in a splendid rite of recovery.

If we make books happen, they make us happen as well. Reading teaches receptivity, Keats's negative capability. It teaches us to receive, in stillness and attentiveness, a voice possessed temporarily, on loan. The speaker lends herself and we do the same, a mutual and ephemeral exchange, like love. Yet unlike love, reading is a pure activity. It will gain us nothing but enchantment of the heart. And as we grow accustomed to receiving books in stillness and attentiveness, so we can grow to receive the world, also possessed temporarily, also enchanting the heart.

Reading gives a context for experience, a myriad of contexts. Not that we will know any better what to do when the time comes, but we will not be taken unawares or in a void. When we are old and have everything stripped away, and grasp the vanity of having had it and of grieving for its loss, yet remain bound in both vanity and grief, hugging the whole rotten package to our hearts in an antic, fierce embrace, we may think, King Lear: this has happened before, I am not in uncharted territory, now is my turn in the great procession.

So much of a child's life is lived for others. We learn what they want us to learn, and show our learning for their gratification. All the reading I did as a child, behind closed doors, sitting on the bed while the darkness fell around me, was an act of reclamation. This and only this I did for myself. This was the way to make my life my own.

R U I N E D   B Y

R E A D I N G

was designed by Anne Chalmers and set by
Wilsted & Taylor, in PostScript versions of
Electra and Copperplate types. The book was
manufactured by Maple-Vail, Binghamton,
New York. The paper on which this book is
printed is acid-free.